Evaluating Your Collection

THE 14 ... EURSHIP

ION

SEUM

I ... NGLAND

Series Editor: *Onie Rollins*

Content Editor: *Onie Rollins*

Copy Editor: *Teresa A. Vivolo*

Designer: *Abby Goldstein*

Manufactured in China by Toppan Printing Company

Library of Congress Cataloging-in-Publication Data

Evaluating your collection : the 14 points of connoisseurship / compiled by Dwight P. Lanmon.
p. cm. -- (The Winterthur decorative arts series ; 1)
Includes bibliographical references.
ISBN 0-912724-50-1
1. Collectors and collecting. 2. Collectibles I. Lanmon, Dwight P. II. Series.
AM231.L36 1999
790.1'32--dc21 98-43759
CIP

Charles F. Montgomery (1910–78)

This book is dedicated to the memory of Charles F. Montgomery, who imparted his enthusiasm for understanding and admiring the products of gifted people who are long gone but whose spectacular creations we still treasure today.

TABLE OF CONTENTS

PREFACE

Collecting antiques has never been a more popular pastime for Americans. Antiques shows abound. They attract large numbers of avid collectors who drive countless miles, arise at odd hours just to be first in line when a show opens, and spend billions of dollars annually.

Henry Francis du Pont (1880–1969), the founder of Winterthur, was a tireless collector. Dealers in the 1930s and 1940s affectionately called du Pont "Mr. Big" because of the scale of his collecting interests. On average, he purchased more than one thousand objects every year for more than forty-five years.

Du Pont's interest in American antiques began in the early 1920s, when there were few serious collectors and just a handful of museums that displayed decorative arts. One such collection was the American Wing of the Metropolitan Museum of Art in New York City. It was du Pont's ultimate model. Eventually, he installed and displayed his collection in the family home, Winterthur, located near Wilmington, Delaware. He called Winterthur his "American Wing."

Du Pont aimed at assembling a comprehensive collection that would document life in America from the early seventeenth century through the mid nineteenth century and lead to an appreciation of the extraordinary skill of American craftsmen. He was buying at a time when numerous important objects were sold, and he was able to acquire many that today are considered masterpieces. When du Pont died in 1969, the museum he founded held some fifty thousand objects; today the collection numbers more than eighty-four thousand.

Considered category by category, the Winterthur collection is rich. The objects made of brass and other copper alloys have been called the most important collection of its kind and date range. American Queen Anne and Chippendale furniture is also well represented, and the textiles, carpets, and needlework are among the best anywhere. These specialized collections serve as resources for this book; unless otherwise noted, all objects illustrated are from Winterthur.

The Winterthur collection is not, however, limited to masterpieces or even genuine objects. Du Pont bought in great quantities but not without care. He was constantly advised by collectors, dealers, and scholars about what to buy. Because of a lack of advanced scholarship in many areas and the changing state of knowledge, however, he inevitably acquired a few extensively reworked and even fake pieces. Over the years, the Winterthur collection has been studied, and problem pieces have gradually been removed. Rather than being discarded, many have been retained to form a study collection—a practice that had du Pont's enthusiastic support—and many items have since been acquired specifically to add to its comprehensiveness.

Du Pont continued to live in his family home, surrounded by his collections, until 1951, when Winterthur became a museum. Even then, he wanted every room in his home to continue to seem "lived in." From the start, he had paneling and other woodwork and stonework from historic buildings installed at Winterthur. He then added furniture that related to the style of architecture in each of the 175 "period rooms" that he created. In each setting, he preferred to use antique fabrics for upholstery and window hangings of the same date as the furniture; the chandeliers, carpets, paintings, and flower containers are also contemporary with other objects in the room *(fig. 1)*.

The earliest period rooms are from mid seventeenth-century New England, and they contain furniture, ceramics, metals, textiles, and other belongings of the first English settlers in the American colonies. Later rooms are furnished in styles that have been classified according to the names of English monarchs, such as William and Mary and Queen Anne, and English furniture designers, such as Chippendale, Hepplewhite, and Sheraton. The neoclassical style, called *federal* in America, is also represented. The collection range ends with objects made in the 1840s and 1850s in the styles reflecting the romantic revivals of classical, rococo, Gothic, and Egyptian tastes.

Many of the rooms at Winterthur express Anglo-American aristocratic taste, but there are also interiors representative of other cultural groups in early America. Pennsylvania German arts and crafts as well as Shaker productions—which document the spare lifestyle and products of the members of the celibate religious commu-

FIG. 1. PORT ROYAL PARLOR

Port Royal Parlor is one of Winterthur's most impressive rooms. Although it contains numerous masterpieces of Philadelphia Chippendale furniture, no single object dominates the space. Achieving this sense of harmony was one of Henry Francis du Pont's criteria for furnishing a room.

nities that flourished throughout New England, New York, and Ohio from the late eighteenth century well into the nineteenth century—are also included *(fig. 2)*.

In addition to outstanding decorative arts objects, there is an unparalleled research library at Winterthur that houses more than 500,000 documents, photographs, and publications. Included are a manuscript and rare book collection; a reference collection on American history, art history, and culture that is second to none; and a photographic archive of documented American decorative arts.

The museum is surrounded by some 966 acres of rolling hills, clear streams, towering stands of trees, and a magnificent naturalistic garden—all part of the Winterthur estate that three generations of du Ponts lovingly nurtured throughout the years. Henry Francis du Pont's dedication to the development of the garden at

FIG. 2. SHAKER DWELLING ROOM

The austere, spare style of the Shaker Dwelling Room presents a stark contrast to the opulence of Port Royal Parlor. The mustard-color painted woodwork dates from the 1840s and was originally installed in a Shaker building in Enfield, New Hampshire.

Winterthur is clearly evident in his unparalleled creation, which thousands come to visit each year.

Winterthur has sponsored formal education programs since 1952. Charles F. Montgomery, the museum's first director, was an influential and charismatic teacher of a generation of curators and historians of American material culture in the Winterthur Program in Early American Culture. Those who were fortunate to learn from him were captivated by his love for objects. One of his favorite questions to raise in debates about the aesthetic merit of a particular object was "Does it sing?" That question continues to be a pertinent and useful one for connoisseurs. Montgomery attempted to build and codify a system for educating the eye and appraising the quality of an object. His approach was summarized in an article on connoisseurship in the little-known 1961 Walpole Society *Note Book*. It has long been felt that Montgomery's system deserves wider recognition. His article, with additions by Winterthur's curators, conservators, and educators, is the basis of this present volume on evaluating objects using Montgomery's fourteen points of connoisseurship.

Dwight P. Lanmon
Director and C.E.O.
Winterthur Museum, Garden & Library

INTRODUCTION

What Is Connoisseurship?

How does a collector recognize "the best"? Simply stated, that is the goal of "connoisseurship," no matter what the subject: needlework, wine, cars, teapots, or cigars. Identifying and separating something that is superior to its look-alikes can be fun, intellectually stimulating, and, occasionally, even financially rewarding. Wine lovers, for example, carefully cruise racks of bottles that look nearly identical to the uninitiated; but, to a connoisseur, the subtle difference of just one year may mean something great, delicious, and valuable; something near-great; or something practically worthless and undrinkable.

Collectors of all media engage in connoisseurship, sometimes intuitively. For example, baseball card collectors have classified and catalogued hundreds of thousands of varieties. One particular card, however, is generally considered to be the most valuable and desirable—that depicting the great Pittsburgh Pirates infielder Honus Wagner. One baseball card may look like another to the uninterested, but the differences in value to a dedicated and informed collector may be startling. Many cards in this popular collecting field sell for pennies each, but the finest known example of a Wagner card sold at auction in 1991 for $451,000 and again in 1996 for $640,500—a world-record price for any sports card. The condition of the top-selling card was pristine. Condition is critical, and creases, tears, and wear diminish value. Every collecting field is plagued with fakes and invisible repairs, so it is essential to know every detail of a genuine card.

Why bother becoming a connoisseur? The obvious answer is to make smart decisions and to avoid being duped. But it is also stimulating and enjoyable to endeavor to *understand* an object and its maker and to have the skills necessary to identify objects that are better than others. Whatever the urge, becoming a connoisseur is not an easy, learn-by-the-numbers task. It takes time and determination. It begins with reading, handling, and studying as much as possible—endlessly. For Charles Montgomery, becoming a connoisseur was a lifelong quest:

> *The primary personal attribute for the connoisseur of decorative arts, as of fine arts, is a good visual memory stored with an infinite number of images of ordinary, fine, and superior objects mentally pigeonholed as to desirability. The connoisseur remembers published photographs of objects and the facts connected with them.*

He must also "learn to see, and then he must look and look and look, and remember what he sees."

The greatest test for a connoisseur comes with a new discovery. Perhaps it occurs at an antiques show, a flea market, an auction, or even in a family member's house. The immediate reaction is that luck has struck, at last! Montgomery wrote that

> *during the first flush of excitement over a new discovery, as in the initial stages of love, the true collector is off on a cloud—his senses hazy. This is the time when the spirit of inquiry and attitude of mind are major assets. The true connoisseur will cultivate habits of skepticism, humility, and objectivity. He will avoid avarice and flee like the plague the desire to get a great bargain. Instead of leaping to conclusions, he will be skeptical. Remembering that "pride goeth before a fall," the wise connoisseur will also exercise the virtue of humility. The humble collector will not, like a peacock, parade his knowledge before the seller and in so doing stop the flow of information that might be had for the asking, or court the reactions always engendered by the "know it all." Finally, the quality of objectivity becomes all-important as the connoisseur attempts an evaluation of what appears to be a prize. To do this, he must establish a number of facts: the approximate date, and the place where the object was made. Obviously he hopes to ascertain the author, though all too often this is impossible. He tries to evaluate the excellence of workmanship, the condition, and*

the effect of wear and tear. To the objective collector, historical evidence will be less important than it is to the cultural historian, though more often than not he will be fascinated by early ownership—in some cases, almost as much as he may be captured by the appeal of the object as a work of magic, the magic of hand and mind sometimes called craftsmanship, but in reality art.

Ways to examine and "rate" an object are demonstrated in the following chapters. While the objects illustrating the approaches are primarily drawn from the Winterthur collection, any collection with two or more similar objects could serve. Indeed, that is the value of this approach: Montgomery's system is applicable to any collecting field. Specifically, the criteria that are used are: overall appearance, form, ornament, materials, finish, color, craft techniques, trade practices, function, style, attribution, history of ownership, condition, and evaluation. Some criteria assume greater importance than others, depending upon the type of object. For example, the *condition* of a piece of early American furniture recently has become more critical than practically any other consideration. However, using all the criteria helps us to understand objects better and to evaluate them objectively.

These criteria are universally applicable, but the conclusions reached in any comparison will not be consistent worldwide. For example, eighteenth-century English furniture often has very different proportions and exhibits a far different approach to ornament than American furniture of the same period. In comparing an English chair and its American counterpart, the judgment of which example is the more "successful" will differ considerably, depending upon the aesthetic tastes of the people asking the question. Therefore, keep in mind constantly that the comments in this book reflect an American aesthetic and that what is "pleasing and elegant" to one person may be "provincial and awkward" to another.

Applying the 14 Points of Connoisseurship

In the early 1900s, tobacco and chewing gum companies began producing baseball cards that advertised their products. Honus Wagner (1874–1955) was one of the most popular baseball players at the beginning of the century. He spent seventeen years of his major league baseball career with the Pittsburgh Pirates, and he was among the first dozen players inducted into the National Baseball Hall of Fame in 1936. Because of his popularity, the Piedmont Tobacco Company as well as Sweet Caporal cigarettes (American Tobacco Company) each included a Honus Wagner

Below left and right:

FIG. 3a. HONUS WAGNER BASEBALL CARD

FIG. 3b. REVERSE OF WAGNER CARD

card among a set of baseball cards issued between 1909 and 1911. Wagner is said to have objected to being included, however, so the companies withdrew and destroyed most of the cards with his photo. Today, about fifty are thought to exist. One was sold for a record price at Christie's in New York (January 21, 1996, lot 716). If only one Wagner card existed, condition would have less impact on value; but, because several authentic Wagner cards are known and because some are in near-mint state, prices vary wildly depending upon condition. The card shown in figures 3a and 3b is the one that sold for the record price; it is thought to be in the best condition of all surviving Wagner cards. The example

FIG. 4. HONUS WAGNER BASEBALL CARD

in figure 4, on the other hand, is damaged: the card is creased, the corners are worn, there is a chip in the upper right-hand corner, and a few pin holes pierce the card. It sold at auction for far less (Leland's, November 20–21, 1993, lot 593).

Condition was the critical factor in understanding why such a high price was paid. However, there is much to be gained by analyzing the cards using all fourteen points of connoisseurship.

1. **OVERALL APPEARANCE**: The appearance is vastly different; one card unanimously would be judged significantly superior to the other.
2. **FORM**: They are both of the same, rectangular form.
3. **ORNAMENT**: They were printed on both sides; both cards bear the same picture on the front, but the one in figure 3 has a printed advertisement for Piedmont Tobacco Company, while the other advertises Sweet Caporal cigarettes. The former is much rarer. To ensure that one is not a copy, microscopic comparison of the printing would be advisable. Reference to an authentic card that is documented would be required.
4. **MATERIALS**: Both are made from the same materials; each is printed on a thin, flat sheet of cardboard. Scientific examination of the card stock would help make certain that one or both are not forgeries that have been printed on similar but chemically different cardboard.
5. **FINISH**: The cards had the same finish when they were printed; apparently neither has been restored.
6. **COLOR**: The color on both cards is similar, but one has lost its crispness due to wear and tear. Cards like these would certainly fade in the sun, but such a concern is an uncommon problem in this collecting field. Because they were issued in

sets and stored in boxes and drawers, most baseball cards are not faded, although they often show signs of handling. Noticeable fading and other damage decreases the value of a card significantly.

7. **CRAFT TECHNIQUES**: Both cards were printed by lithography. Any color photocopy of a Honus Wagner card would, by definition, be a copy.

8. **TRADE PRACTICES**: Cards depicting popular sports heroes were enclosed in cigarette and chewing gum packs beginning in the early twentieth century. The idea of collecting complete sets was encouraged. The Honus Wagner card was one of a set of 150 subjects.

9. **FUNCTION**: These cards were made to enhance sales of cigarettes. Only one or two of the known Wagner cards advertise Piedmont cigarettes, while the others advertise Sweet Caporal cigarettes.

10. **STYLE**: Judging by the way Wagner's hair is parted in the middle, by the Pittsburgh Pirates uniform, and by the advertising information on the back, the date of these cards is consistent with other baseball cards printed in the early twentieth century. They were issued about 1910.

11. **ATTRIBUTION**: The name of the printer is not inscribed on the card, but the name of the tobacco company for which one of the cards was made—Piedmont—and the brand name of the cigarettes that the other card advertises—Sweet Caporal—are printed on the back.

12. **HISTORY OF OWNERSHIP**: The early history of these particular cards is unknown. The card that sold for the record price is said to have been discovered about ten years ago in the archives of a printer, but that history has not been documented.

13. **CONDITION**: The example shown in figure 3 has survived without any apparent damage. Its history of ownership helps explain why it is in mint condition. The other card has suffered damage.

14. **EVALUATION**: The card in figure 3 is in the finest condition of all known Honus Wagner cards; it sold at auction for $640,500, while that depicted in figure 4 sold for $55,000. In assessing the authenticity of a unique object or a rare variation of an object that was produced in sets, it is critical to compare the unique version to common examples. For example, among Honus Wagner cards, only one known example (possibly two) has the Piedmont advertisement; it would be advisable to compare the printed Piedmont advertisement to the same advertisement on other cards from the same set before concluding that the unique version is authentic. Because fakers understand that collectors prize rarity, they focus on producing unique objects rather than common ones.

CONCLUSION: Both cards are authentic, and both were printed about 1910. To collectors, the card in figure 3 is vastly more desirable than the other; indeed, it is the most valuable of all sports cards. Restoration of the example in figure 4 would enhance its appearance but probably would not increase its value significantly.

CHAPTER I

Overall Appearance

When first looking at an object, it is important to let oneself go and try to get a sensual reaction to it. I ask myself: Do I enjoy it? Does it automatically ring true? Does it sing to me?

CHARLES F. MONTGOMERY

When you find a new object and you find yourself saying "yes!"—stop, and while you are trying to conceal your emotions, take a deep breath and look, really look, at it. Ask yourself, does it "work"? Does the ornament complement the form? Are the lines pleasing and in accord with the style? Is it graceful? Does the object have unity? What is the relationship of masses and voids? What about the harmony of the whole and the integration of the parts? Unity is a thing of subtlety; yet, more often than not it is a prime factor in differentiating the work of a master from that of a follower. Did the craftsman deviate from the norm to such a degree that it is a new conception and more interesting? Pencil sketching is frequently an excellent way to "see" both details and overall line.

Connoisseurs often sense these factors instinctively without stopping to analyze them, but the points should also be established objectively. When an object appears to violate the rules for a particular form made in a given place and time, its authenticity may be questioned.

The subtlety and importance of understanding the design concept of *unity* is emphasized by the three chairs shown here. Together, they seem to suggest that a gradual evolution of design occurred from the curvilinear Queen Anne style to the more elaborate Chippendale style in Philadelphia between about 1730 and 1790. All three were once considered to be among the furniture masterpieces at Winterthur. Today, not all are considered to be masterpieces, and one is thought to be a fake that uses some old parts and some new.

The Point in Practice

Three related chairs illustrate the importance of design unity (*figs.* 5–7). The overall composition of the chair in figure 5, made of walnut, is based on harmonious, flowing, curved lines and smooth, solid forms.

Does the design succeed? Note how the rear posts echo the outline of the splat, creating birdlike forms in the empty spaces between. The shells on the crest rail and the knees are not added

but carved from a solid piece of wood; they contribute to the elegance of the chair, as do the S-curved, or cabriole, legs. The chair looks as if it would be very comfortable; the splat and the rear posts are subtly shaped in a curve that fits the back. Furthermore, the quality of its design, carving, and wood, and its excellent condition make it a desirable example of the Queen Anne style, as interpreted in Philadelphia between 1730 and 1760.

The mahogany chair in figure 7 was also made in Philadelphia. It is in the style known as Chippendale, which was fashionable from the 1750s to the 1780s. It differs from the Queen Anne chair in having an angular seat, a pierced splat, a crest rail that projects over the rear posts, and S-curved legs ending in ball-and-claw feet. The composition is built up of intersecting curved and straight lines and busy, carved surfaces.

Does it succeed? The answer depends largely upon personal taste. This chair reflects an aesthetic style that is different from that of the Queen Anne chair. It is richly carved; some would find it too

Left to right:
Fig. 5. Queen Anne side chair
Fig. 6. Transitional side chair
Fig. 7. Chippendale side chair

ornate. But, note how the carving flows logically from the crest rail, down the splat and stiles, and how it relates to the carving on the seat and front legs. The unity of this design and the quality of the carving are noteworthy. Mahogany is a very dense, hard wood. As can be seen here, it may be carved crisply. In addition, the color of the wood enhances the visual richness of the chair.

The chair in figure 6 mixes elements found in the two other chairs. It might be called transitional—halfway between the Queen Anne and Chippendale styles. It has curved rear posts, a curved seat, and S-curved legs—all characteristic of the Queen Anne style. But it also has a bowed crest rail that projects over the rear posts and a pierced splat characteristic of Chippendale chairs. The wood is mahogany.

The amount of carving on the chair in figure 6 would be considered desirable by a collector, and a transitional chair would be of the utmost rarity. Indeed, there is no other chair like it known. However, the features of this chair are not combined successfully to form an integrated composition. Does the carving on the crest rail relate to that on the posts or splat? Does the carved decoration enhance the object, or does it overwhelm it? Does the quality of the carving compare with that on the Chippendale chair? The answer to every question is no. Was the maker simply a poor designer, or was he a later workman concocting a chair that never existed in the eighteenth century? Or, was a mid eighteenth-century Philadelphia Queen Anne chair altered significantly in the early 1900s? The greasy, dark, opaque finish of the chair suggests that alterations were hidden intentionally.

This chair is now believed to have been constructed early in the twentieth century from parts of a genuine Queen Anne chair and embellished with elaborate carving and a Chippendale crest rail.

The logical integration of design and decoration is usually a potent indicator of the quality—as well as authenticity—of an object.

CHAPTER 2

Form

Form, more than any other quality, distinguishes a work of art. Conception and proportion give it nobility and distinction. . . . Overall measurements and in some cases those of individual parts are necessary to establish the norm and general proportions. They are vital as a part of the record and for making comparisons with related pieces, especially through photographs.

CHARLES F. MONTGOMERY

Form is defined as an object's shape and mass and the proportion of its parts. The shape of an object and the relationship among its parts may reveal its maker's time, place, and cultural background. Similar objects made at the same time but in different locations will often look different because they reflect different cultural influences and consumer expectations.

In handmade objects, slight differences in size and detail are expected—but within limits that varied with the maker's ability. Among the hand-formed products of American glass factories, for example, there is remarkable uniformity within each factory's production.

Artisans who master their craft tend to become habitual in the way they execute functional details. For example, a glassmaker who makes pitchers for a living must produce an object that pours well and is strong enough to be picked up by the handle. Once this is mastered, the handles that a glassmaker produces tend to look the same, and the form of the spout tends to be repeated as well. Consequently, it is sometimes possible to distinguish objects made by different makers by comparing the forms of handles and spouts.

Measurements of individual parts may reveal information concerning the age of an object and repairs that have been made to it. Weighing a piece of silver provides a basis for comparing the present weight with the original weight, which was frequently scratched on the bottom of the object by the silversmith. Some reduction in the weight of a tankard or mug, for example, might be expected from wear and polishing. But a difference of more than an ounce or so should make you suspicious about possible repairs or alterations that might affect the form of the object.

The Point in Practice

Pitchers like these were popular in America in the 1820s and 1830s. Both were patterned in hinged molds with similar geometric designs. The footed pitcher *(fig. 8)* would be considered rare and desirable by collectors of early American glass; the other pitcher *(fig. 9)*, on the other hand, is a relatively common form.

The forms of the handles and spouts indicate that they were made by different glassmakers, each according to a different mental image of what "proper" handles and spouts should look like. That only one of these pitchers was really made to function as a pitcher is an important conclusion that may be drawn from studying the forms of the handles and spouts.

The pitcher in figure 8 has a visually and functionally "weak" handle and spout. The upper attachment of the smooth handle is small and extends only slightly down the neck; the lower attachment has a small pincered ridge above the end, which lies close to the body. The rim of the pitcher is flat and circular, and the spout is pulled slightly downward.

The handle of the pitcher in figure 9 is thick and ribbed. The upper attachment is massive and extends nearly to the shoul-

Above left and right:
FIG. 8. PITCHER
FIG. 9. PITCHER

der of the jug. The lower end is long and was pincered elaborately into two ridges, drawn out, and rolled back to form a decorative loop. The spout was formed by pushing the sides of the rim up and pulling the point boldly downward.

This pitcher was made as a functional object. The handle is meant to support the weight of the pitcher when it is full, whereas the handle of the other might crack at the top or bottom because the attachments are so small. The spout of the pitcher on the right is a no-nonsense, functional spout. It is intended to direct poured liquid but cut the flow efficiently without dribbling. The pitcher on the left, however, with its shallow spout, would dribble and create a wide liquid flow.

The pitcher in figure 9 probably dates from the 1820s or 1830s and was made to be a functional jug. The footed pitcher *(fig. 8)* was created as a fake in the 1920s. Because it was probably made to be sold to a collector, it had no functional use, so it did not matter if the spout or handle "worked" or not.

FIG. 10.
TANKARD/PITCHER

In the nineteenth century, and especially during Prohibition in the early twentieth century when their use as drinking vessels declined, many eighteenth-century tankards were converted into pitchers by adding spouts. That is what happened here: the side of the tankard was pierced with numerous holes, and a spout was soldered in place *(fig. 10)*.

How can you tell if an object's form has been altered? In the case of silver, many silversmiths inscribed the original weight of an item on the bottom of the piece. If there is a scratched weight or if that weight might be found in an estate inventory, it can be compared with the present weight of the object, indicating that changes have been made. Compositional analysis of the body, cover, and spout—that is, a scientific examination of the materials used to make the tankard—would confirm that the spout was made using a different, purer, modern alloy.

CHAPTER 3

Ornament

I ask myself: Was the ornament used to cover up structural features that might otherwise be unattractive? Or was it used to highlight and emphasize certain elements or features? Ornament provides punctuation and, at its best, gives not only pattern and rhythm, but also unity to the composition.

CHARLES F. MONTGOMERY

Color, figure (as in wood), texture, turning, carving, engraving, enameling, painting, appliqué, printed design, and a hundred other means have been employed to attain ornamental effects. For each, ask yourself: Why is it there? Does it accomplish its purpose? Is the overall effect better for its presence? Ornament is usually secondary to form and should heighten its effect rather than obscure it. The type and amount of ornament is determined by the skill of the craftsman, the financial resources of the consumer, and the tastes and preferences of both. Ornament often helps to identify an object's style, place of origin, and relative merit. Ornament that is poorly integrated may be suspect, since adding ornament to a plain object is an easy way to increase its market value.

To evaluate the effectiveness and quality of ornament, it is essential to be acquainted with the types of ornament used and the heights of technical excellence achieved by artisans in a variety of times and places, working in the style of the object in question.

One of the most dramatic, important, and valuable forms of furniture made in America in the eighteenth century is known as "blockfront." The name derives from the projecting and receding drawer fronts on the objects. Popular in New England, blockfront furniture was made in Massachusetts, Rhode Island, and some areas of Connecticut from about 1730 to 1790.

Connecticut and Rhode Island blockfront chests were sometimes embellished with carved shells. The two shell-carved, blockfront chests shown in figures 11 and 12 were probably made in Connecticut. One is a typical (not to say common) example of eighteenth-century design and craftsmanship, while the other is unique. How does the ornament compare? Does one composition make more sense than the other? Do the shells add to the overall unity of the design, or do they detract from it? One chest was made about 1770–90; the other was probably made in the late nineteenth century with the intent to deceive. Which is which?

Glassmakers in eighteenth- and early nineteenth-century America usually produced functional objects such as bottles and windows. Befitting their purpose—to contain and transport liquids safely—most bottles were not decorated. If they were meant to be decorative as well, glassmakers used brightly colored glass and molded patterns. Individual mold characteristics, particularly defects in the molds used to produce decoration, make it easier to group similar objects and identify makers and dates.

Pocket bottles were common in eighteenth-century America. They were mainly meant to hold liquor, and, as the name implies, they were pocket-size. One merchant in Hartford, Connecticut, advertised in 1790 that he had glass pocket bottles "suitable to carry the comfort of life into the fields."

Pennsylvania glassmaker Henry William Stiegel (1729–85) recorded making as many as fifteen hundred pocket bottles per month in his Manheim factory. No pocket bottles can be positively identified as being made there, but many examples in colored and colorless glass discovered in the region have generally been accepted as Stiegel products because of their similar form and decorative patterns.

Four pocket bottles attributed to Stiegel and decorated in a molded pattern described as "diamond daisy" are illustrated in figure 13. These exhibit the entire range of colors associated with Stiegel: amethyst (the most common color), blue, and colorless. The flasks share not only a similar decorative pattern but also the same compressed globular shape and proportion—except for the one at the far right. It has a very different shape, being flatter and more pear shaped.

Mold defects that are shared on three of the bottles suggest that they came from the same mold, and possibly the same factory. The fourth flask was patterned in a different mold; no other pocket bottle in this exact pattern is known. Is it a rare variant? Could it be a fake? Judging by its different form and proportion, it is evident that it was not made by the glassblower who fashioned the other three bottles.

The Point in Practice

The four-drawer chest in figure 11 has the expected number of shells in the usual place—three on the top drawer. The middle shell is concave and carved into the drawer front while the two outer shells are convex and applied, or glued on. The line of the blocking on the drawer fronts is carried smoothly from top to bottom. The refined decoration, called gadrooning, along the lower edge echoes the scale of the fine fluting within the center shell. It is a well-crafted and well–thought-out piece that was produced by an artisan who understood the "architecture" of the blockfront style.

The three-drawer chest in figure 12 is the only known example with nine shells. The concept is also very different. The middle shells are not completely concave; they project slightly on the two lower drawers, and their carving is shallow by eighteenth-century standards.

These facts as well as some construction differences and obvious unexplainable "damages" lead to the conclusion that the nine-shell chest is a modern object made of old wood. The cabinetmaker, a determined faker who undertook the fabrication, may have been working from photographs but did not adequately understand the detailing of blockfront furniture with shells.

The modern reputation of Connecticut furniture as being quirky and individualistic is what permitted this chest to be

Fig. 11.
Chest of drawers with three shells

Fig. 12.
Chest of drawers with nine shells

Fig. 13.
Pocket bottles

accepted as genuine for decades. When du Pont bought the nine-shell chest in 1929, it had a long history of ownership. The chest and its "history" were both fraudulent.

All these pocket bottles were once attributed to Henry William Stiegel's Manheim, Pennsylvania, glasshouse, and they were thought to have been made between 1769 and 1774 *(fig. 13)*. The attribution of one, however, has been changed radically.

Three were made in a mold that gave each flask an identical pattern of stylized florets in diamonds. There are five diamonds in each horizontal row. Also, because of tiny scratches in the mold that were transferred to the glass along with the pattern, it is clear that all three were made in the *same* mold (not just an identical one) at Stiegel's factory.

The fourth flask *(fig. 13, far right)*, on the other hand, was patterned in a different mold; it has six diamonds in a horizontal row. Other differences become apparent upon closer examination of this flask. The neck is straighter and less flared, the shoulder is sloped rather than rounded, and the body is less globular and more tapered. The other flasks differ slightly in size from one another, but they do not vary much in shape and proportion.

All these details suggest that caution should be exercised in attributing the fourth pocket bottle to Stiegel's glasshouse. The flask on the far right is probably a fake made in Czechoslovakia between about 1915 and 1930 with the intention of deceiving American collectors. The moldmaker probably only had a photograph of a genuine Stiegel pocket bottle to copy, and no one realized (or then cared) that the number of diamonds was different. The glassmaker also did not understand the proportion typical of Stiegel pocket bottles. Instead, he produced a copy with all of the elements but none of the details of form and proportion of authentic pieces.

CHAPTER 4

Materials

In this step, the goal is to gather and assess information on the individual constituents such as woods, textile fibers, pigments, metals, and fasteners (wherever possible, I make observations in direct sunlight).

CHARLES F. MONTGOMERY

Identifying materials is a critical step in understanding an object. A single object may contain many different materials. For example, woods, surface coatings, adhesives, hardware, and textiles were chosen by furnituremakers on the basis of appearance, strength, workability, cost, availability, and the dictates of fashion. Knowing what is typical for objects made in a particular place and time is important when trying to identify when and where an object was made.

Instruments that are commonly available and that may be helpful in making the most accurate as possible observations about materials include a magnifying glass, camera (for a permanent record; occasionally, ultraviolet and infrared light photography may also be useful), microscope, and ultraviolet lamp. X-ray photographs of some objects often reveal important information, although the equipment may be more difficult to find and use. (Doctors, hospitals, and some museum laboratories may take X-ray photographs for a fee.) On occasion, the connoisseur may also wish to invest in the services of an analytical laboratory.

Accurate information on the exact components of an object, combined with knowledge of the history of technology, often provides definitive evidence for dating and attribution. The value of knowledge of the history of technology, for instance, is evident in the study of pigments. The use of Prussian blue on an object establishes that the layer of paint could not possibly have been applied prior to 1704, when this artificial pigment was developed. Similarly, the presence of titanium in the decoration of a group of "ancient" Chinese vases led to the exposure of the entire group as forgeries since titanium is a twentieth-century discovery. Today, the microscopic identification of woods in furniture is a boon in determining the origin of furniture, since cabinetmakers were accustomed to using woods native to their locality for the interior parts of their cabinetwork.

Craftsmen chose materials that were best suited to the task at hand, but the specific woods used changed over time. Illogical choices evident in a piece of eighteenth- or early nineteenth-century furniture, such as the use of expensive mahogany for drawer sides or elaborate carving done in pine, should make the examiner question the object's authenticity. In studying seventeenth-century furniture, it is important to know that maple, an excellent choice for turning, was often painted to imitate ebony. Discovery of turnings in mahogany or ebony on a seventeenth-century American chest should sound an alarm; although they are fine woods for turning, craftsmen rarely used them. Pine, an inexpensive wood, was used frequently for drawer sides in the eighteenth and nineteenth centuries; in the seventeenth century, on the other hand, oak was used more often.

Walnut was the most fashionable wood for American Queen Anne furniture (1725–60), but mahogany was more popular for furniture made in the Chippendale style (1750–90). Mahogany was used especially for furniture with carved decorations; maple and pine do not carve so well and, consequently, were used less often for elaborately carved cabinetwork. Many imported, exotic woods were used in the nineteenth century, including rosewood.

Oak, the most popular wood of the seventeenth century, was rarely if ever used for high-style furniture during the eighteenth and early nineteenth centuries. At the end of the nineteenth century, however, when medieval and Renaissance furniture styles were revived, oak became popular again.

A knowledge of the history of the popularity of certain woods helps to identify which of the two chairs shown in figures 14 and 15 is the later copy. The earlier chair is made of mahogany, while the later one, made of oak, is a product of the colonial revival era in the late 1800s. The materials of these two chairs are a principal aid in drawing this conclusion, although differences in proportions and carving are also helpful.

Historically, it is rare to link contemporary evidence about an eighteenth-century American object with the surviving piece. Such evidence was used, however, to determine that a silver caster, or shaker, was not what it seemed to be. A problem was identified upon reference to the historical record. The application of the principles of connoisseurship suggested that one part might not be original, and compositional analysis of its materials proved that the suspicions and explanation were well founded. Case closed!

The Point in Practice

Compare these two chairs *(figs. 14, 15)*. Their basic features identify them as belonging to the Chippendale style, which was fashionable during the second half of the eighteenth century. There are significant differences between them, however. Look closely. The one in figure 14 is made of oak, which has a coarse figure and texture, is pale in color, and can be extremely difficult to carve. The strong grain is visible through the dark stain that was used to make it look like mahogany and to appear more like its eighteenth-century counterpart. The chair is also too tall and narrow by eighteenth-century standards. The carving has been done in part by machine, and it is crude by comparison. The leaves on the knees are thick and lack the refinement of eighteenth-century carving, and the ball-and-claw feet are clumsy.

The chair in figure 15, on the other hand, is characteristic of the best Philadelphia mahogany furniture of the 1760s and 1770s. Mahogany, with its fine, dense grain, carves well; it was very expensive in the mid to late eighteenth century, so this chair would have been displayed in the best parlor or chamber. Observe how the carved leaves on the crest rail move elegantly down and onto the strapwork splat. Likewise, the raised beading along the edge of the front seat rail flows smoothly onto the knee blocks

Fig. 14a.
Oak side chair

Fig. 14b.
Detail of oak side chair

FIG. 15.
MAHOGANY SIDE CHAIR

and into the edges of the cabriole legs. The carving of foliage on the knees is crisp and delicate, and the ball-and-claw feet are boldly sculpted. The finesse of line and proportion and the elegance and appropriateness of the carved decoration combine to make this a masterpiece of Philadelphia Chippendale furniture.

FIG. 16. CASTER

A knowledge of material helped to determine that this silver caster had undergone changes *(fig. 16)*. It was owned by Nicholas Bayard (1698–1765) and was listed in the inventory of his estate prepared in 1766.

The weight of the caster was also listed in the inventory, as 3 ounces 13 pennyweight. Today, however, it weighs only 2 ounces 20 pennyweight 21 3/4 grains. Wear and polishing would reduce the net weight somewhat, but a difference of nearly 17 percent of its original weight seems too much. What accounts for the excessive decrease? Two explanations were possible: either this was not the caster listed in the inventory or something had been removed or replaced on the piece. Upon closer examination, the piercing in the cover seemed crude, so the caster was submitted to compositional analysis. The result was the discovery that the silver used to make the cover was very different from that used in the body and the handle; it was highly refined and could only have been made after 1870. The purity of the silver used to make the body and the handle was, however, consistent with eighteenth-century alloys. The compositional analysis of the materials led to the conclusion that the cover is a replacement and that it is lighter than the original one.

CHAPTER 5

Finish

Connoisseurs, curators, and conservators have different opinions about the degree to which an object should be treated. Some prefer surfaces "in the rough," with no restoration. Others prefer to perform minimal, reversible treatments. Still others want their objects restored to look as they did when they were new.

WINTERTHUR CURATORS

There probably is no more controversial area of connoisseurship than the question of finish, in part because what "original" means is frequently a matter of conjecture and subjective debate.

Furnituremakers apply resin coatings to make surfaces shiny, enhance the color and grain of the wood, and protect it. Over time, the appearance of the initial finish coat will change due to use, accumulated dirt and grime, and later applications of polish, wax, or more finish. The finish may deteriorate, change color, or degrade from shiny to matte, crazed, and peeling. In addition, an original surface may be more than just one layer. A painted and gilded chair in the Winterthur collection, for example, was found to possess seven original layers, and two more were recently applied on top of them. Sometimes the finish can be restored to a close approximation of its original appearance. A carefully restored early finish can retain a desirable appearance when dirt and grime are selectively removed. On the other hand, a refinished object can lose its character—and much of its value—through the removal of early finishes.

One side to the refinishing versus original surface controversy is demonstrated by two two-hundred-year-old bureau tables. Looks can be deceiving. At first glance, the bureau in figure 17 appears to be an abused, old war horse, while that in figure 18 looks like a three-year-old filly ready for the Kentucky Derby. One has an old, irregular, crusty finish, while the other is even and shiny. There seems to be little question as to which would be considered more valuable today. In fact, both bureaus are magnificent; yet, a careful comparison yields several important differences in form, decoration, construction, and finish—differences that affected their price when they were sold at auction in 1996.

Admittedly, the price of an object at auction is not always an accurate indicator of its value. To reach a record price, two people must want the object (more or less) equally and have similar abilities to pay. Marketing plays a role as well. However, what appeals to one collector may not appeal equally to another, and tastes do change. In January 1996, perhaps having two similar, great Newport shell-carved blockfront bureaus on the market at the same time was a matter of one too many. Perhaps the comparison between the two caused a wider shift in sentiment than might otherwise have been the case. One appears to be an early version of the blocked and shell-carved bureau, while the other is a mature version that demonstrates the ultimate perfection of the form. In addition, it is certainly true that today many American furniture collectors are attracted passionately to pieces that have old, dirty finishes. That has not always been so; Henry Francis du Pont and the museum staff that succeeded him often refinished and polished furniture at Winterthur. Their attitude reflected collecting tastes of their time and of English and Continental collectors, whose polished, shiny, refinished pieces were (and to a certain extent still are) the norm. Aggressively stripping finish from an object certainly can diminish its appearance and its importance if the work is not done carefully and sensitively. But, in the hands of a competent conservator, repairs may be made and finishes renewed that enhance an object. It is important to know, therefore, precisely what work has been done—and why. And, it is critical to understand in advance what refinishing might do to the value of a particular piece. Removing a finish that appears to be original may diminish the value of an object significantly, but living with such a piece may be very challenging.

Original finishes are sometimes mistakenly cleaned as a result of misunderstanding the original intent and interpreting it as deterioration. An elaborate copper rococo teakettle and stand appears to be heavily tarnished, and it might be tempting to polish it to a lustrous glow. However, in this case, it would diminish the value of the object significantly, for the dark brown patina is the original surface finish.

What and what not to polish is an age-old question for collectors. In metals, the answers vary, but the current taste is generally for polishing. For silver tableware and hollowware, the intention is to have it look new. Beware, however, of chemical dips, which may leave a white, frosted appearance. For brass drawer pulls and lighting fixtures such as candlesticks, "as new" is typically the desire unless the brass has decorative finishes, including gilding. Be especially cautious in polishing nineteenth-century brass lamps and candlesticks, for the decoration is often in a varnish layer, which would be lost. For coins and medals, polishing is never acceptable. For pewter, light burnishing with fine 0000 steel wool is fashionable; if there is active pewter "disease," it is best to turn to a specialist to remove it. In the case of bronze, not polishing is the norm; many bronzes were patinated to develop the dark brown or green color. Rust is usually removed from iron, but a black surface is generally left alone; a mechanically buffed "silvery" look is not desirable on cast or wrought iron. Gold and gold-coated (such as bronze doré) objects generally need no more than washing, as they rarely tarnish.

The best answer to "should I clean or not?" is to seek the advice of a conservator or curator. Polishing removes part of the history of the object, and it may not be replaceable. And, perhaps even more important, polishing, cleaning, or refinishing can significantly diminish the value and importance of an object, while leaving it alone rarely endangers it.

The Point in Practice

Newport chests of drawers with recessed kneeholes and blocked and shell-carved drawers are widely considered to be masterpieces of American furniture design. Fewer than fifty examples are known, and most are signed by or are attributed to cabinetmakers in Newport, Rhode Island—principally members of the

Townsend and Goddard families. These chests were made between about 1750 and 1780 *(figs. 17, 18)*.

The bureau in figure 17 has been described as having "remained continuously in untouched condition, without even surface treatment, and therefore remains original in all respects, including color and patination" (Parke-Bernet Galleries, New York, "The Notable Americana Collection of Mr. and Mrs. Norvin H. Green" [November 29–December 2, 1950], lot 663). It retains a worn, old finish that has never been touched by a scraper or paint remover. It is in the condition that many advanced collectors today admire—and are prepared to pay a lot for. On the other hand, earlier collectors valued a more "as new" look, which led them to remove such deteriorated, old finishes. The bureau in figure 18 has been refinished, and there has been some minor restoration.

The bureau in figure 17 looks as if it has had a much "harder" life than that shown in figure 18. Underneath the deteriorated finish, however, is a piece that has had very little damage and no restoration. In addition, its stunning carving, the striking balance and rhythm of its sculpted shells, the delicacy of the carving within the shells, and the history of ownership going back to the first family that possessed it make the bureau in figure 17 the more coveted and costly. It sold for $3,632,500 at Sotheby's in New York (January 20, 1996, lot 48). The bureau in figure 18, however, sold for only $156,500 at Christie's, New York, just one week later (January 27, 1996, lot 359). Part of the reason for the discrepancy in price is undoubtedly the fact that the Sotheby's bureau table is a classic example of the type and is attributed to Edmund Townsend. The Christie's bureau table, on the other hand, appears to be an early version of the type and is less appreciated in the marketplace.

The dark brown color of the teakettle and stand, which was imported from England in the eighteenth century, seems to hide a

Fig. 17. Bureau table

Fig. 18. Bureau table

FIG. 19. TEAKETTLE, STAND, AND BURNER

lustrous metal underneath, yet this is precisely the appearance desired by the maker and original client *(fig. 19)*. The piece is made of copper, and it has been intentionally patinated to look like bronze and to resist tarnish. The patination process involved soaking the finished pot in a bath of sulphur, potash, and water and heating it until the desired color was reached. This finish could be removed by polishing, and it is remarkable that this pot, burner, and stand have survived with the original dark brown patination. Removing that patination would certainly diminish its desirability.

CHAPTER 6

Color

Here the ideal is to find objects with original color showing as little fading or discoloration as possible.

CHARLES F. MONTGOMERY

Because an object's finish changes over time, color changes too. Old objects show color variations caused by use and exposure to air, atmospheric pollutants, and sunlight. Mottled surfaces, darker and lighter sections, and many scratches are expected on objects that have been used for hundreds of years.

When eighteenth-century objects survive in unfaded condition, the colors frequently seem garish to us today. These are rare survivors, whether printed cottons, patterned silks, embroidered pictures, wallpaper, or painted furniture. They are prizes to be sought out, just as one seeks the jewel-like clarity in the colors of porcelain or pottery.

Many facts of technology concerning color achievement offer clues to dating. For instance, it was impossible to print true green on textiles until the nineteenth century. Prior to that time, green was obtained by applying yellow over blue.

Organic dyes are among the most unstable and likely to fade. Textiles that are exposed to sunlight are particularly vulnerable, and the rate of change may be shocking. Curtains that are never moved may be found to have startling contrasts between the fabric hidden within the folds and that exposed to the light. Bedhangings and covers that are exposed to direct sunlight, in comparison to a valance or hanging that is shaded, may also develop strong color differences through fading. Although the same happens to needlework, the degradation often goes undetected because the colors fade uniformly across the entire surface. The differences become immediately apparent, however, when the back of a needlework panel can be seen.

Distinguishing natural color change from induced change is critical in determining an object's age and authenticity. Intentional changes in color often occur on pieces made to deceive, and several procedures are legendary. These include such

Fig. 20a. Needlework picture

practices as washing oriental carpets with animal urine to bleach them and mellow their colors, exposing furniture to the elements to fade it, and burying bronzes and ceramics to gain encrustations quickly that look old. Various stains and paints are also sometimes used to suggest antiquity. Stains are usually easily detected, for often they are not uniform and appear in the wrong places.

The Point in Practice

This delightful needlework picture *(figs. 20a, b)* was embroidered by Priscilla Allen in Boston in 1746. She was probably eighteen at

Fig. 20b. Reverse of needlework picture

the time and attending a boarding school for young ladies, where she was taught to read, write, and sew using both useful and fancy needlework. Fancy needlework like this was the work of girls who belonged to families of comfortable financial means, for it was, by definition, nonutilitarian.

Priscilla copied a print—probably a French print called *Le Soir* (evening)—for the pastoral design. She used tent stitches of wool (crewel) thread on a fine canvas backing to depict a woman carrying a basket of flowers and a man playing a flute. She used French knots to create the soft texture of the sheep.

The lady's red dress is the dominant feature of the picture. The background colors have faded into a balanced palette of soft blues, yellows, and creams, which give the red a contrast that it did not originally have. Indeed, the reverse side demonstrates that all of the colors were more vivid and better balanced *(fig. 20b)*. In particular, note the intensity of the yellows and greens, which have disappeared from the front, as well as the burgundy of the man's coat. This difference in color is one indication of the object's age.

Prices for American eighteenth-century fancy needlework have increased dramatically in recent years. Priscilla Allen's picture is striking, early, rare, and important, but it is typical of the state in which most survive. In studying a needlework picture, it is critical to examine the stitches, threads, dyes, and canvas carefully and to compare them with known genuine examples. A reproduction or fake picture will exhibit bright colors. A buyer must exercise caution, however, as it is relatively easy to expose new needlework to sunlight to fade it and make it look old.

A comparison of the appearance of two drawers further illustrates the importance of evaluating color. Note the difference in the color of the interiors of these drawers *(figs. 21, 22)*. The one shown in figure 21 has the even brown color associated with oxidized

FIG. 21. DRAWER FROM A CHAMBER TABLE

FIG. 22. DRAWER FROM A WASHSTAND

softwood (in this case, white pine). The drawer in figure 22 has a smeared, streaky, opaque grayish tone.

On genuine eighteenth-century furniture, the softwood oxidizes to a mellow brownish color, but the extent of oxidation depends on the location of the surface. Oxidation should be consistent with location. (For example, the underside of the bottom drawer of a high chest would logically be a different color than the underside of the top drawer due to one drawer being used more than another and the underside of the top drawer being afforded protection from the elements by the drawers below.) Because the piece in figure 22 was made with new wood and because the cabinetmaker was impatient to wait two hundred years for the wood to acquire a natural aged color, a chemical stain was used to imitate the color of aged wood. The stain produced the immediately recognizable color seen here, which does not come close to what it should be. In addition, there are streaks of color where the stain overlapped. Discovery of the drawer stained to imitate the signs of age prompted further inspection, which revealed that the entire object is new and that it was probably made to deceive an unwary collector.

CHAPTER 7

Craft Techniques

Here the goal is to evaluate (1) the quality of craftsmanship; (2) the techniques and practices employed (and through this study to determine if they are typical of a period, locale, and culture); (3) the personal idiosyncracies of workmanship of the author of signed or documented pieces; (4) the congruency of the parts and whether the whole is by one author or is made up at a later date of two or more antique parts. This study often reveals restoration.

CHARLES F. MONTGOMERY

The phrase "quality of craftsmanship" may seem self-explanatory, but it is important to keep in mind that quality of workmanship within a craft varies widely with time and place. Knowing how an object was made in a given time and place is essential for a connoisseur. Such knowledge can help confirm the object's origins and reveal later alterations.

Furnituremakers used techniques that employed economy of both time and materials. When an artisan found a technique that worked well for him, he tended not to change. Since craft skills were passed down through generations from master craftsmen to apprentices, changes in technique evolved slowly. In the eighteenth century, some artisans worked with a high degree of naturalism, their products rivaling nature in fluidity and artistry; others achieved successful results with less skill, using abstract ornament and simplified form. Contrast, for example, the products of city and country cabinetmakers. One might employ costly imported woods and the services of a specialist carver; the other might use maple or pine, with limited decoration. Neither version is inherently better or worse than the other; rather, each reflects different attitudes and cultural backgrounds as well as different craft traditions and training.

Characteristics for most objects fall into a pattern and more often than not are peculiar to a particular area. The phenomenon of such regional characteristics of objects is widely recognized and is one with which every connoisseur must be thoroughly familiar.

The connoisseur of furniture must also learn to spot the telltale marks that tools leave, for they are sure indicators of technology, and they are very helpful in identifying a maker (based on comparisons). The advent of the circular saw, which was patented in England in 1777 and was first produced in America in 1814, for example, made woodworking much easier, and it was adopted rapidly. The saw leaves an immediately recognizable mark, with curved, parallel lines running across the surface. It is visually different from the marks left by a handsaw or a modern band saw. Therefore, the discovery of any modern power-tool marks on the wood in a piece of furniture supposedly from the eighteenth century should cause alarm. If the questionable parts are not replacements, then the entire object must date after the latest technological feature.

The cost and difficulty of obtaining tools was significant until the end of the nineteenth century, when mass production and more efficient transportation made them more widely available. Sometimes tools changed hands a number of times before wearing out, and they were often used by several generations of artisans and at many different locations. Owners of glass factories, for example, counted their metal tools and molds as important assets, and they sold them when they went out of business. Today, many glass factories still own and use molds from other factories.

Other craftsmen, such as pewterers, were equally protective of their molds. Each mold was made of bronze or brass, and each required a considerable investment. Pewterers were inventive in using the same molds to produce different objects, which can then be identified as a particular pewterer's work, whether they are marked or not.

Fig. 23. *Left to right:* Flagon, coffeepot, coffeepot

There is, however, one important factor to remember in the quest to identify objects on the basis of specific molds: old molds still exist and may be used, and new molds may be taken from genuine examples of eighteenth-century pewter. Two plates, bearing two marks of Thomas Danforth III of Rocky Hill, Connecticut, when he was working in Philadelphia (about 1800–1818), were discovered several years ago in Pennsylvania. They looked authentic. However, they both had been produced in a new mold. What gave them away was the fact that both plates had the same maker's marks in precisely the same location. This would be impossible if the plates were authentic and had been individually marked with the maker's stamps. When the fake mold was made, it not only copied the shape of the original plates but also duplicated the marks. If the plates had been sold separately, they might never have been detected.

Caution and knowledge of the characteristics of authentic antique American and European pewter and period craft techniques remain the best defense against fraud. In short, connoisseurship is essential.

The Point in Practice

Complex objects made of pewter cannot be formed by hammering or turning on a lathe. Consequently, each object must have a full-size mold to form it, or it must be possible to solder together parts from separate molds to form a larger piece.

One of the most famous pewterers who worked in the eighteenth century in Philadelphia was William Will (1742–98). The two coffeepots shown in figure 23 bear Will's mark and, with the exception of the platform base and spouts, were made with the same molds. Measurements of each part demonstrate that they are identical. Ten separate molds were used to make both: one mold each for the finial, cover, hinge, upper body, lower body, and handle sockets and two molds each for the feet and spouts. After molding, the pots were soldered together and turned. Beading was added to emphasize the molded bands and conceal the joints.

The flagon *(fig. 23, left)* is not marked, but it may be attributed to Will on the basis of part-for-part comparisons with the marked coffeepots. The cover, hinge, upper body, lower body, and foot were made in the same molds as those used for the coffeepots. Additional molds were needed for the flagon's spout, thumbpiece, and handle. The same handle mold was also used on marked tankards and mugs by Will.

This practice of comparing the craft techniques evident in an undocumented piece with those of an object that *is* documented to a particular maker is one that can be applied to any medium.

Fig. 24. Plates

Precise molds that will replicate minute details have been developed for a number of products, from jewelry to dentures. Similar mold materials may also be used for criminal purposes, including producing exact fakes, such as the pewter above *(fig. 24)*.

These two plates were probably made with a mold taken from an authentic pewter plate made by Thomas Danforth in Philadelphia. The rim molding is weak, and the weight is a bit heavier than typical, but they are otherwise very convincing. The two marks that Danforth used are clearly evident on the backs. Surprisingly, they are in precisely the same location on each plate. Since marks were not on the molds but rather were punched by hand and because they are not decorative elements, it is highly unlikely that two separate marks would appear in exactly the same location on two plates and in the same relationship to each other. In addition to identical marks, even the scratches on these plates appear in the same places—which would be impossible if the plates were genuine. There is only one interpretation: they are fakes.

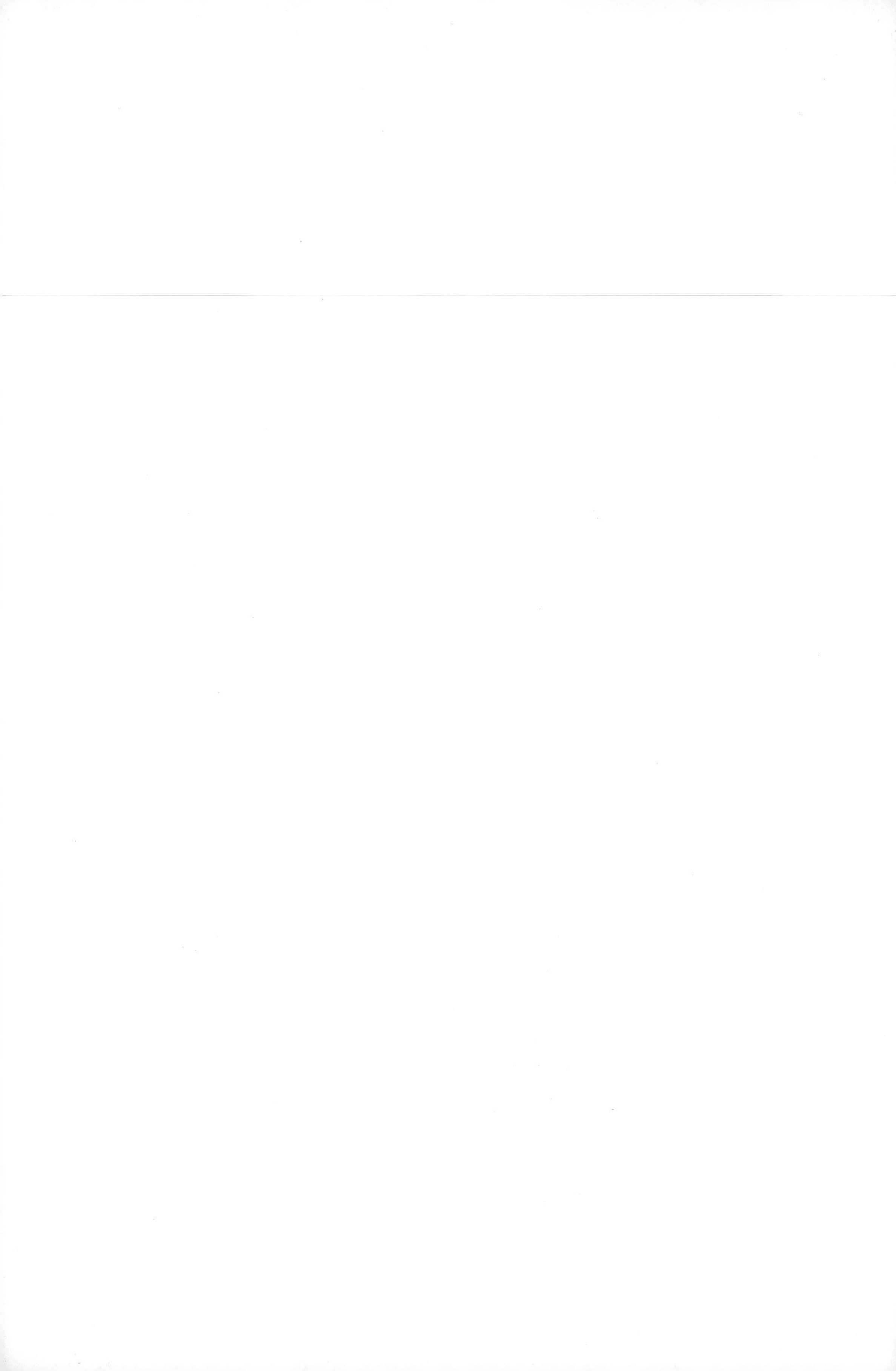

CHAPTER 8

Trade Practices

Trade practices often reveal valuable information. The branded name of the maker, while common in French furniture, is, like the label, seldom encountered in English cabinet wares; yet both are quite occasionally met in the American product. Therefore, one would be much more wary about a labeled piece of English furniture than he would about an American piece.

CHARLES F. MONTGOMERY

Trade laws are often overlooked as sources of valuable information about craft objects. Hallmarking on silver was regulated in England to hold silversmiths accountable for the quality of silver and, at times, for proving that taxes had been paid. Collectors of English silver have long used hallmarks to establish the date of manufacture and to identify makers—which relates to the original purpose of the system, if not its intent. No such system was required in the American colonies, so a means of precisely dating American-made silver objects is lacking. Many American silversmiths identified their products with stamps incorporating their initials or names, but a mark was not required by law. One consequence for collectors of American silver is that an English-style piece without a maker's mark is more likely to be American than English.

Excise and tariff laws also resulted in practices that inadvertently assist connoisseurs in dating objects. The McKinley Tariff Act of 1891 required that new objects imported into the United States be marked with the country of manufacture. Therefore, something marked "Made in France," for example, was made after 1891. Similarly, an English law of 1776 that remained in effect until 1811 offered export rebates to English manufacturers of cotton cloth if they wove three blue lines into the selvage. Therefore, any piece of white cotton cloth that contains three blue lines in the selvage is of English manufacture and was woven between those years.

The organization of the crafts also had considerable impact on the appearance of products. For example, in American cities in the eighteenth century, craftsmen from different trades often worked together to produce a single piece of furniture. Such collaboration speeded production and assured a high level of quality. Often an upholsterer or cabinetmaker established the design and specifications for an object and then contracted with specialists for production of the parts. Understanding the collaborative process helps a connoisseur recognize the evidence left by different hands working on a single object. That is one reason why various pieces in a set may not share the same details of construction or carving.

In addition, in the eighteenth and nineteenth centuries, craftsmen not only produced and marketed their own products but also sold, and often imported, the work of others. An example is the Grecian couch illustrated in figure 25. It bears the printed paper label of a Salem, Massachusetts, cabinetmaker, who advertised "Cabinet work of all kinds / MADE AND SOLD BY / Thomas Needham, / Charter Street, Salem." For decades, the couch was accepted as Needham's work. However, that is no longer the case.

Prints, too, were often the work of many artists. In the case of illustrated books published in the eighteenth and nineteenth centuries, three or more artists could have been involved: first an artist would create a painting; an engraved copper plate would then be produced of the painting, perhaps by a second artist; it would then be printed by a third specialist; and, if the illustrations were to be colored, a watercolorist would tint them. This was the case for one of the most elegant botanical books ever published *(fig. 26)*.

Knowledge of trade practices may enhance the appreciation of an object; it may also provide evidence for dating, attributing, and authenticating it.

The Point in Practice

This 1820 Grecian couch *(fig. 25)* was once thought to be the work of Thomas Needham, Jr., of Salem, Massachusetts, because it bears his printed paper label. Made in a form that was fashionable in France at the beginning of the nineteenth century, the couch reflects the widespread interest in classical archaeology.

Recognized as being unusual for Salem furniture in its use of caning, the couch is now believed to have been made in China for export to the West. The materials and construction are typical of Chinese pieces. And Needham is known to have been involved in the China trade. He may have imported and sold this couch; the label states that cabinetwork was "made and sold" by him. Needham was but one of many merchants who were involved in the lucrative trade with the Orient.

Artist Philip Reinagle painted *Tulips (fig. 26)*, which became one of the most famous plates in Robert John Thornton's *New Illustration of the Sexual System of Carolus von Linnaeus . . . and the Temple of Flora . . . Being Picturesque, Botanical, Coloured Plates of Selected Plants . . . with Descriptions.* The book was a scientific compendium of the revolutionary botanical classification system arranged by Linnaeus. The floral plates that Thornton

Fig. 25. Couch

Fig. 26. *Tulips,* Engraved by Richard Earlom from Robert John Thornton, *Temple of Flora* (London, 1807)

commissioned from several artists have assured his posthumous fame.

Reinagle has depicted "Rembrandt" tulips against a background intended to evoke their source in the Netherlands; a windmill is shown at the right. The painting was engraved in mezzotint by Richard Earlom. The plate was printed in brown and blue inks, and the luscious watercolors were added by hand. Its color is very fresh, and the book itself is wonderfully preserved.

CHAPTER 9

Function

The study of function ought to lead us to the understanding of basic character as well as give us the reason for an object's existence. . . . Why was this object made? What were the limiting conditions imposed by materials, techniques, and skills? What was the intent of the artist?

Charles F. Montgomery

The function of an object determines its reason for existence. Sometimes, important clues to authenticity may be gleaned from observations of functional qualities. Can the object have adequately performed the uses for which it was intended? If an object cannot reasonably fulfill its apparent function, its authenticity may be questioned. However, function can change over time. For example, a piece of furniture may be made obsolete by changing fashions and new technologies, at which point it may be modified to serve a new function. Connoisseurs look for evidence of such changes as they try to determine the age of an object.

It is important also to understand the evidence of wear and tear on an object as it relates to function. Does wear occur where one would expect it if the object had been used as designed? For instance, does the dent made by the thumbpiece on a tankard lid come at just the right spot on the tankard handle? Does the wear on the rung of a chair occur at the point where it was natural to rest the feet?

A glass teapot is an object that seems to defy logic. Anyone who has immersed glass in boiling water knows that it tends to crack or shatter. Today, glass teapots and coffeepots are made of heat-resistant glass that withstands the shock of boiling water, but it is highly unlikely that the teapot in figure 27 (made of lead glass) would have withstood such use. Is it a fake because it would never have survived use? Perhaps not.

The function of miniature furniture made in the eighteenth century has been debated extensively. Pieces such as the tiny high chest of drawers shown in figure 28 are often described as "salesman's samples," implying that cabinetmakers produced pint-size versions and carted them across the country to interest clients in ordering a full-size one. The argument becomes especially strong when the miniature is a piece of the quality of this example; without the knowledge that it stands less than thirty-three inches tall, it would be difficult to judge its true scale. Unfortunately, the suggestion that such pieces were salesmen's samples is rarely supported by documentary evidence. There are better explanations.

The Point in Practice

This three-footed glass teapot and cover imitate the form and size of teapots made in many other materials, principally silver and ceramics, in England around the middle of the eighteenth century *(fig. 27)*. The three curved pad feet are impressed with lions' masks and paw feet, common on teapots. The shape of the body is what collectors call a "bullet" shape, after the spherical form of a musket ball. The body is pierced with several holes to form a strainer where the spout is attached. The cover has a hole to permit steam to escape.

Glass teawares are rare today, perhaps because they failed to survive much use. No one has had the temerity to pour boiling water in this teapot to test it for fear that it would break. As a consequence of its implied uselessness, some have questioned its authenticity. There are, however, other known examples from the eighteenth century: two English lead glass teapots and numerous Continental opaque-white glass teapots with matching

FIG. 27. TEAPOT

tea bowls and saucers. Tea sets of "white" (meaning colorless) glass were advertised in Boston in 1732; whether they included teapots in addition to cream jugs, tea caddies, waste bowls, tea bowls, and saucers is unknown. It has also been suggested that this might be a punch pot to hold and serve cold fruit beverages, but that seems implausible given the small size and the presence of the steam vent in the cover. (The lid fits loosely, so the hole is not necessary to prevent a vacuum being formed while pouring.)

On the other hand, such a piece could have been made as a demonstration of ingenuity and ability rather than for a functional purpose. In civic parades in the eighteenth and nineteenth centuries, artisans frequently marched together with their fellow

craftsmen, carrying the most outlandish and fanciful objects they could make. Glassmakers carried long and colorful glass canes and swords, blew fanfares on glass trumpets and hunting horns, fired salutes from glass cannons, and wore glass top hats decorated with glass feathers. Perhaps some also made domestic objects such as teapots to capture attention. After the parade, it would have been understood that the glassmaker would take his handicraft home to amuse and delight his family. So, although this object seems to be nonfunctional for its form, it is believed to be authentic.

There is convincing, adequate wear on the feet, on the bulbous sides of the pot, and on the rim of the lid—just where you would expect to find wear from use—to suggest that this vessel was, indeed, made in the eighteenth century.

In addition to the usually discredited "sample furniture" theory, a common explanation for the purpose of miniature furniture is that it was made for adult collectors or for children. Indeed, there is evidence in the form of letters, diaries, and invoices to support both possibilities. Alternatively, although this miniature high chest *(fig. 28)* lacks a locking device to protect its contents, it may have held small precious items or even spices, which were highly valued in the seventeenth and eighteenth centuries.

Many spice chests are known from the Chester County region of Pennsylvania. There are six known examples in this high-chest form; the other five have either lockable doors enclosing the drawers or locking devices on some of the drawers.

FIG. 28. "SPICE" CHEST

CHAPTER 10

Style

> *The analysis of style involves the study of form, ornament, color, craft techniques, and the weighing of data gained through virtually each of the preceding steps; but it particularly involves a knowledge of function since, in the decorative arts, most objects were made for useful purposes.*
>
> CHARLES F. MONTGOMERY

The distinctive visual features of an object define its style. Specific stylistic features may link an object with a particular period or place of manufacture. For example, some early furniture styles were reintroduced at later times. The newer versions usually can be identified by looking at their stylistic cues, construction techniques, and choice of materials.

A knowledge of function can equip the connoisseur to understand objects better within their social setting, but a knowledge of the development of styles will enable the connoisseur to analyze an object within a stylistic frame of reference, gauge its quality, and estimate its date more accurately. A knowledge of European prototypes as well as various products of the same period and purpose is critical, as is the ability to evaluate American products against European standards.

The development of furniture styles in New England from about 1650 to 1800 is shown here. These objects illustrate the adherence of New England colonists and artisans to English styles, and they show how styles changed over a span of 150 years. A similar sequence selected from any East Coast, English-speaking urban area of America would demonstrate that the same fashion trends waxed and waned in the same order and at approximately the same rate.

A similar progression may be seen in wineglasses made during the same 150-year period. The design of drinking glasses reflected the latest styles in furniture and interior decoration—as did all of the other decorative arts.

A wide knowledge of style enhances the enjoyment of an object and provides a framework and basis for comparing and understanding how the piece relates to interiors and attitudes of the time. Distinguishing between the genuine and the imitation can also frequently depend upon knowledge of style.

The Point in Practice

Five armchairs demonstrate how fashion and style changed in New England over a period spanning only about seven generations, or 150 years *(figs. 29–33)*.

The first chair *(fig. 29)*, from Boston, reflects the style known as *Jacobean* in England; in America, it is identified as *seventeenth century* or "*Pilgrim Century.*" Although there are chairs of this period that are made entirely of joined planks of wood, it is immediately apparent that the most important craft in producing this particular chair is turning. Not a single board was used in its construction. It is made of a collection of turned spindles, held together with mortise-and-tenon joints to produce a stable seat. In the 1650 to 1675 period in the colonies, few such chairs were made. They were meant to impress; comfort was provided by a woven split-ash seat and often a thickly stuffed, fabric-covered cushion.

Comfort increased in seating furniture as wealth—and standards of living—increased in New England. The second chair *(fig. 30)* reflects a late seventeenth-century fashion in England. Called *William and Mary* by American collectors, the style shows a Dutch influence on English furniture at the end of the seventeenth century and on American furniture into the early eighteenth century. World trade was increasing, and the availability of cane from China made this new upholstery form possible and popular. The woven cane seat provided a degree of comfort unknown before—cooler in summer and slightly forgiving—although the seat was probably always accompanied by a stuffed fabric cushion.

The wood frames of these William and Mary chairs were also elegant and decorative. The elaborate crest was often carved and pierced, and sometimes the stretcher between the front legs was carved in a similar pattern. Here, the stretcher is turned, and there are bold turnings on the legs and arm posts. The legs end in what were called *Spanish* or *brush* feet. An armchair

Below left and right:
Fig. 29. Pilgrim Century great chair
Fig. 30. William and Mary armchair

such as this was also meant to impress and to enhance the dignity of the person seated in it.

The third chair *(fig. 31)* reflects the exotic influence of China. Armchairs with curved, spoon-shape backs that cradled and supported the sitter were being made in China by the early seventeenth century. Some Chinese furniture reached Europe and influenced cabinet- and chairmakers, who imitated the lines of the imports. The spoon-shape back and the curved rear posts and crest on this chair reflect a Chinese chair fairly faithfully. This chair is more comfortable than either of the previous chairs, and the seat, being stuffed and upholstered, adds to that comfort. We call it *Queen Anne* style.

The fourth chair *(fig. 32)* is an example of an English *Chippendale* or *rococo* style. The differences from the Queen Anne

Left to right:
FIG. 31.
QUEEN ANNE ARMCHAIR
FIG. 32.
CHIPPENDALE ARMCHAIR
FIG. 33.
NEOCLASSICAL ARMCHAIR

chair are immediately obvious. The crest extends over the rear posts, the back is flatter than on the Queen Anne chair and is pierced, and the S-shape legs have ball-and-claw feet.

While the transition between Queen Anne and Chippendale may have been dramatic, the change to the neoclassical style was even more startling, as furniture designers turned to classical antiquity for designs of form and decoration. The fifth chair *(fig. 33)* is in the neoclassical taste; the urn back indicates its ancient origin. In England such a chair would be called *Hepplewhite,* after the designer, while in America we term it *federal,* in recognition of the political ambitions of the newly independent United States. The design for this chair is modeled on one in George Hepplewhite's *Cabinet-Maker and Upholsterer's Guide,* which was published in London in 1788. Design books and imported objects brought to America helped inform local craftsmen how to produce the latest London fashions for American clients.

Five drinking glasses *(fig. 34)* echo the style changes shown in the illustration of New England armchairs. Glasses such as these could have been found in the same households as those chairs, when they were new. The changes in style were limited mainly to the stems.

The earliest glass of the five, on the far left, is thin and fragile. It was made in Venice and looks almost too delicate to have been used with furniture such as figure 29. But colorful stuffed fabric cushions, often used on such chairs, would have contributed to the richness of the setting and the appropriateness of the glass.

In the seventeenth century, Venetian glass was considered the most fashionable among wealthy Englishmen and English colonists. Glass made in England around the middle of the seventeenth century reflected the Venetian style, but little of it was exported to the American colonies.

A new type of glass, *lead* glass, incorporating lead oxide in the mix, was developed in England in 1674. The lead added weight and brilliance, and a wineglass bowl rang brilliantly when tapped. Lead crystal soon became the most popular and fashionable glass throughout the English-speaking world.

Wineglasses made of lead glass and dating from the end of the seventeenth century and beginning of the eighteenth are recognized by their bold, turned stem forms, as can be seen in the next example to the right. Similar turnings are found on tables and chairs in the William and Mary style, as in figure 30, for example. The massive construction of the stems showed off the brilliance of the new lead glass to perfection. These glasses, termed *heavy baluster* by collectors, are prized as a classic marriage of material and form, each contributing to the other.

Fig. 34.
Drinking glasses

Typical stem forms are based on furniture elements and architectural features of the period.

The third, middle, glass is more restrained in the form of its stem than the glass to its left, and the lighter stem suggests the refined curves of the chair in figure 31. In a 1753 treatise on aesthetics, "The Analysis of Beauty," William Hogarth termed this S-shape, seen in the legs of the Queen Anne chair and the wineglass stem, "the line of beauty."

The rococo style is reflected in the elaborate twist within the stem of the fourth glass and the delicately enameled grapevine on the bowl. The twists are made of minute threads of opaque white glass. Twist-stem glasses must have been wonderful additions to a candlelit dining table that featured elaborate and colorful ceramic dinner services and silver flatware.

The fifth glass, on the far right, reflects the neoclassical taste. The main decoration is facet cutting on the stem and polished floral cutting and engraving on the bowl. The stem imitates the flat, reflective surfaces on the furniture, and the polished engraved decoration imitates the delicate carving that can be seen on the neoclassical, or federal, chair in figure 33.

CHAPTER II

Attribution

On signatures:

For signatures of any type, the observer must determine whether the signature is actually that of the author applied at the time of manufacture; or an authentic label or mark (stamped with an old die) applied at a later date to an unmarked piece; or a fraudulent inscription or signature of some type applied to an unmarked example by a forger.

On stylistic attribution:

One of the most difficult aspects of connoisseurship is to make sound attributions on the basis of style. . . . Are they by a particular hand? Or are they copies or adaptations from his atelier? Or are they the work of a forger?

CHARLES F. MONTGOMERY

Signatures on crafts produced in America include everything from handwritten inscriptions in ink, chalk, and pencil to engraved, scratched, burned, stenciled, or stamped names and initials and printed paper labels. Whatever the mark, the connoisseur exercises skepticism about the authenticity until it has been proven. In addition, equating signatures with authorship is not always wise or justified; owners and retailers who had nothing to do with making an object sometimes applied their own identifying marks.

It is relatively easy to put a paper label on an object to suggest authenticity and increase value. Some old, authentic paper labels that were never used do exist, but most labels that have been applied recently are newly printed. Occasionally, fakers find plain, old paper of the proper age to use, making the new labels difficult to identify; fakes on new paper should be easier to separate from the authentic. The examination of a label on an object should aim at identifying the paper type, the printing process, the adhesive, and how long that piece of paper has been on the piece.

The identification of stylistic similarities also helps distinguish the work of Pennsylvania German potters, who signed few of their products. These craftsmen emigrated from the Germanic states of Europe to America, where they produced decorative and functional pottery that emulated what they and their customers were used to; later potters, trained as apprentices, continued making the same styles and forms.

In addition to producing functional kitchen- and tablewares, some Pennsylvania German potters made elaborately decorated "show" pieces that demonstrated their mastery. Among the most valuable are large plates with scratched (or *sgraffito*) decoration. Although only a few pieces of Pennsylvania sgraffito are signed, there is enough consistency in potters' individual work to permit the attribution of some unsigned examples.

The Point in Practice

In 1990 Winterthur acquired a handsome side chair dating from the 1850s, featuring an unusual rope-carved back *(fig. 35)*. The most desirable aspect of the chair was that it bore a rare label of J. H. Belter and Company at 552 Broadway, New York City *(fig. 36)*. The chair was significant because it was one of the few known pieces bearing that particular label and because it was one of only four known Belter chairs that did not have a laminated back.

John Henry Belter perfected the production of elaborately carved, laminated wood furniture. Because of the lush carving

FIG. 35. SIDE CHAIR

FIG. 36.
LABEL ON SIDE CHAIR

and richly colored and figured woods (often rosewood), Belter furniture has risen dramatically in collectors' appreciation—and value—in the past two decades.

There was one troubling aspect about the label, however: it was different from another, accepted style of label that Belter used while at the 552 Broadway address. That discovery prompted the curatorial and conservation staff to scrutinize the label, and several interesting discoveries were made:

- The paper is a pale brown color, with mottled staining associated mainly with the bleeding of the ink;
- The label is rippled, following the rough saw cuts on the inside of the chair frame, but there is no abrasion or grime on the raised areas, and there is no wear on the edges (abrasion and dirt would be expected since the chair had been reupholstered several times);
- The irregular edges of the label were probably cut with a knife or scissors, but the edges are lighter in color (they have not discolored at the same rate as the paper's surface, and stains have not carried down through the edges);
- Adhesive laps over one edge, showing that the edge was trimmed before the label was applied;
- Under ultraviolet light, the adhesive on the label fluoresces a bluish-white, while the adhesive on other parts of the chair fluoresces a yellowish color;
- Analysis shows that the adhesive used for the label was a polyvinyl acetate, or PVA (such as Elmer's Glue, which is a twentieth-century adhesive), while that used in assembling the chair was an animal glue;

- The label was printed on a softwood-pulp paper with fibers identifiable of the spruce/hemlock family; the mix showed fibers that were pulped mechanically and by an unbleached sulfite pulping process that was not begun until the 1880s.

As a result of these discoveries, it was concluded that the label was fake. The chair is authentic and dates from the 1850s, but it cannot be attributed to Belter.

Large, red clay dishes were sometimes elaborately decorated with slip, a white clay diluted with water to a creamlike consistency that was coated uniformly on the dish. After the slip dried, the coating was scratched to form complex designs in a technique called *sgraffito* (Italian, meaning *to scratch*). The entire face of the dish was then covered with a lead glaze, and sometimes copper salts were sprinkled on it to create green splotches. After firing, the glaze formed a durable, glossy layer that protected the decoration. Such dishes were likely made for show, not for use. Today they are collectors' prizes, and authentic examples that can be associated with some of the better-known potters bring tens of thousands of dollars.

The dish in figure 37 was made and signed by George Hübener, a potter working in the latter part of the eighteenth century in Upper Hanover Township, Montgomery County, Pennsylvania. Hübener decorated the dish with an elaborate sgraffito two-headed eagle (an imperial German motif). The necks diverge and are decorated with short dashes to indicate feathers. The bird's heart-shape breast with scalelike decoration is divided by a pointed oval decorated with dashes. The wings are raised and also decorated with dashes; the tail feathers are spread; the legs and feet are indicated by lines. There are stylized tulips at either side, and there is a four-petal flower with feathery foliage

FIG. 37. SGRAFFITO PLATE

FIG. 38. SGRAFFITO PLATE

above. The date "1786" and the initials "GH" of George Hübener are in the central panel, above and beside the bird.

An inscription runs in a band around the edge: "Cadarina Raederin Ihre schüssel / Aus der ehrt mit ver stant macht der Haefner aller hand" [Cadarina Raeder her dish / From the earth with sense the potter makes everything].

The dish in figure 38 also bears a double-headed eagle. The decorative details are similar to those on the signed Hübener dish, except for the stylized floral sprays on the breast and the more delicate tail feathers, which look almost like those on a peacock's tail. At either side of the heads are two flowers that are very similar to Hübener's, and the sprays of foliage below are also similar. Features not found on the signed dish are the preening peacocks at either side of the eagle. There is an inscription between the bird's heads, "Hir ist Abgebilt / ein dabelter / Adler" [Here is pictured a spread eagle]. Another inscription, a version of the Biblical "Golden Rule," runs around the rim: "Susanna Steltz: ihre schüssel: Alles was ihr wolt das euch die Leute duhn sollen das duth ihr ihnen, Merz 5th 1789" [Susanna Steltz her dish. Do unto others as you would have them do unto you. March 5th 1789].

Fig. 39. Sgraffito plate

The dish in figure 39 also shares many characteristics with the signed Hübener dish: the tulips, sprays of foliage with small oval leaves, four-petal flowers with feathery foliage, and scale-decorated breast on the preening peacock. The attributed Hübener dish shares the preening peacock with dash-outlined tail feathers and the four-petal flowers. The inscription, "Wann das maenngen und das hengen nicht wehr, so staenden die wiegen und hickel heusser Lehr: September 14th 1787" [Were there no men (for women) or roosters (for the hens) left empty would be cradles and also chicken pens: September 14th 1787], is similar in letter form to the inscriptions on both dishes. Note, for example, the similarity of the capital letter *S* on the two unsigned dishes *(figs. 38, 39)* and the word *schüssel* on the dishes in figures 37 and 38.

In order to make reasonable attributions, it is necessary to find close links between designs and construction. These three dishes were made within a period of only three years and exhibit very close similarities. Those similarities support the attribution of the two unsigned pieces to George Hübener.

CHAPTER 12

History of Ownership

Documentation through sales and exhibition catalogues or family history is a well-known method and device for authentication. Such history can provide valuable information as well as an aura of authenticity; but here skepticism should be the byword. I constantly ask myself: "Is such documentation logical? Are there gaps in the history? Are there implausible assumptions?"

CHARLES F. MONTGOMERY

It is a wise connoisseur who regards the history of an object and its ownership as supporting, rather than primary, data. There are certain obvious exceptions, such as signatures, bookplates, and shelf marks on books that may be regarded as virtually irrefutable indications of early ownership. Otherwise, it is safest to consider whether the history is at all plausible.

Family histories, whether written or oral, are notoriously unreliable. Rarely is the intent malicious. Mistakes usually result from faulty memories. Stories that have bases in fact become distorted with repetition, and they sometimes become associated with the wrong objects. Furthermore, family dating of objects is frequently muddled with the age of the person owning it. How many times has the story been heard that an object belonged to a great-grandmother who died at a very advanced age? The faulty conclusion that sometimes follows is that the object must be very old—at least as old as the deceased owner.

Can any family histories be trusted? Yes, they can, especially when the history is written around the time that the incident took place.

For example, imagine that you are offered an unusual chair that was probably made on Long Island some time before the middle of the eighteenth century. On the back is an engraved copper plaque: "George Washington used this chair when he dined at the home of Zebulon Ketcham on April 21, 1790 at Huntington South (now Amityville) Long Island." The initials "I*C" are inlaid prominently on the crest rail. The chair no longer belongs to Ketcham descendants, but its ownership can be traced to a doctor to whom it was given by a grateful patient who was a descendant. How reliable is the history? How would you go about assessing it?

Few objects dating from the eighteenth century survive with "complete" documentation of who made them, when, where, for whom, and why. A rare exception, and an important object, is illustrated here. It is one of a set of six matching tankards made by the Boston silversmith and patriot Paul Revere. Any piece of silver made by Revere is rare and valuable, so it is very important to find out if the set of six tankards is authentic. Confirming its history of ownership can help.

The Point in Practice

This chair *(fig. 40)* was accompanied by an engraved plate stating that George Washington sat in it in 1790. It is a spectacular and rare form and is in relatively good shape for a chair that was more than fifty years old by the time Washington is supposed to have used it. Microscopic examination identifies the woods used in the chair as American-grown and confirms that all the parts, except the finials, are original. According to family tradition, the original owner was Jacob Conkling (1676/77–1754), or his son Israel (1719–77), of South Huntington, Long Island; Israel's daughter, Hannah, married Zebulon Ketcham of Huntington. So far, so good.

Fig. 40. Armchair

Because of its good condition, it is evident that the chair was cherished and preserved as something special, but could a plaque engraved more than one hundred years after an historic event be accurate? Fortunately, more information is available to confirm the family history. In a diary kept by George Washington, he noted on April 21, 1790, "We dined at one Ketcham's which had also been a public house, but was now a private one." If not proof that this chair was actually used by Washington, at least it is certain that the owners of this chair entertained the president. The history seems sound.

Figure 41 and five other tankards matching it bear a lengthy inscription documenting that they were donated by Mary Bartlett to the Third Church in Brookfield, Massachusetts. Mary Pape had married Ephraim Bartlett in 1732; when he died in 1761, he left his entire estate to his widow, who later bequeathed two-thirds to the church for the purchase of silver vessels. Although the tankards were not procured from Revere until 1772, they are engraved "The Gift of Mary Bartlett Widow of Eph^{m} Bartlett, to the third Church in Brookfeild. 1768."

The hallmark on each tankard is "REVERE" within a rectangle. This is a recognized mark of Paul Revere, Jr. (1734–1818) of Boston, who produced the largest group of silver objects in this period in America. Many of his business records also survive, including daybooks documenting his work between 1761 and 1797. Under a 1772 entry, Revere lists six "Silver wine Qt Tank^{d}," and he notes their individual weights; those weights correspond with the engraved weights on the set of tankards at Winterthur. It is the only set of six tankards listed in Revere's daybooks.

Expenses noted in Mary Bartlett's estate papers include one for her executor to travel to Boston in 1772 "to Engage the Silver Vessells" and another "to Receive the Vessells." In addition, the executor eventually recorded "Six Silver Tankards

Fig. 41. Tankard (one of a set of six)

Fig. 42. Set of six tankards

D[d] to the third Chh in Brookf[d] agreeable to the will as per their Receipt appears [£] 66.18.1."

Documents such as estate inventories, public records, and personal diaries are all valuable sources of information when attempting to authenticate the history of ownership.

CHAPTER 13

Condition

Evidences of natural aging and wear such as coloration, patina, and softening of edges, corners, and contour are but a few of the attributes of the antique that add fascination to any object. But the thing with which the connoisseur must come to grips is the demerit to be attached to wear, tear, and accidents.

CHARLES F. MONTGOMERY

Practically speaking, the older, rarer, less obtainable, and finer the object, the more restoration, repairs, or blemishes you must be prepared to accept. Connoisseurs must judge independently, however, and set their own criteria.

Condition is critical in identifying superior and more valuable objects. It also helps connoisseurs identify forgeries and restorations. Most wear is gradual, but every object, regardless of its age, should display a logical pattern of wear that corresponds to its use. Some objects survive in miraculously good condition, but most reveal age through naturally occurring wear and tear.

Too little wear may call the age of an object into question. Too much wear can diminish an object's beauty and may erase traces of its workmanship. Major damage severely compromises interest in and the desirability of an object. The amount of wear considered acceptable varies, collector to collector and medium to medium.

Restoration may also diminish the value and importance of an object: skinned surfaces, severe over-restoration or conjectural restoration, and overpainting sometimes reduce the desirability of a piece catastrophically. Many restorations are detected through examination by raking light as well as by X-ray.

On functional objects, such as a child's high chair, it would be natural to assume that considerable wear would be present and that it would occur logically in areas subjected to the greatest abuse. Comparing two Windsor high chairs is illustrative of the value of critically examining wear.

The question of how much wear is acceptable arises frequently. A decision to acquire a piece is usually at issue, and the debate often revolves around questions such as "When will I ever see another?" or "Have I ever seen another in better condition?" If the object is unique, the question may become "Can I live with it in this condition?" In the case of mass-produced but handmade objects, there are few that are truly unique. Some may be much rarer than others, but there is little doubt that another related example will turn up someday. In this case, a connoisseur may be pickier. Consider the question of two tin coffeepots. How would you rank them?

The Point in Practice

One of these high chairs was made between 1765 and 1810, while the other was made between 1920 and 1935 *(figs. 43, 44)*. Which is which? Examining patterns of wear helps identify them.

Look at each chair, especially at their seats and arms. One has allover yellow paint with black banding and ornamental gilding; it is not original, but it probably was applied more than one hundred years ago *(fig. 43)*. The edge of the seat has been worn smooth, and the paint is abraded all over. It is about the amount of wear that would be expected on a chair that has been used by squirming children for more than a century. Also, by looking closely, you can see that a great deal of grime has accumulated around the joints.

The other chair has its original green paint *(fig. 44)*. Surprisingly, two spindles in the back have no paint, but others retain all of their paint. Look at the seat; there is no evidence of

Above left and right:

Fig. 43. Windsor high chair

Fig. 44. Windsor high chair

wear, and there is little accumulated grime. On the other hand, there is considerable wear on the stretcher, although it is much too far down for a child to have scraped it.

The chair shown in figure 43 is a genuine late eighteenth- or early nineteenth-century Windsor high chair, while that in figure 44 is an "aged" interpretation of an eighteenth-century high chair made between 1920 and 1935 at furnituremaker Wallace Nutting's manufactory.

Tinware was inexpensive and widely available in America in the eighteenth and nineteenth centuries. It is actually made of thin sheet iron that has a tin coating to inhibit rusting. Many functional tin objects were left plain, while others were coated on the outside with asphaltum or paint and further decorated with painted ornament in bright colors. Much of it was imported from England, but a great deal was also made here.

FIG. 45. COFFEEPOTS

These two coffeepots are typical of the products of Pennsylvania craftsmen working in the second half of the nineteenth century *(fig. 45)*. One is painted bright red; the other has a typical dark brown asphaltum background. The red pot was used heavily and shows it; there is significant wear on the background and decoration. The decoration on the pot on the right is so well preserved that it appears never to have been used, and its original decoration and surface are nearly pristine.

The brown coffeepot has two interesting inscriptions: "875" and "James H. Robbins Philadelphia" are scratched on the bottom. The first may be a stock or design number; it probably is not an incomplete date, although the coffeepot does date from the 1870s. Robbins may have been the original owner, but sometimes the names of the decorators are inscribed in the same way.

The brown coffeepot is in better condition than the red one, but its color is not nearly as desirable. A rare Pennsylvania example with original red paint and multicolor floral decoration sold at auction for $33,000 in 1997. The same coffeepot in dark brown would probably have brought about one-twentieth the price.

Which would you choose? There is no correct answer; the decision is a matter of taste, collecting focus, standards—and wealth.

CHAPTER 14

Evaluation

The ultimate goal in studying any object . . . is to answer the question: How good or how bad is it in terms of (1) beauty or aesthetic value; (2) intrinsic value in terms of materials and long hours of skillful fashioning; (3) extrinsic value in terms of association, ownership, or competition? The connoisseur must ask himself: Is it important as a thing of beauty? Is it rare, typical, or illustrative of the culture that produced it? Is it worthy of purchase? And, if so, at what price?

CHARLES F. MONTGOMERY

One function of connoisseurship is arriving at objective conclusions based on the examination of objects and knowledge of period practices. Another is making value judgments about the relative artistic merit of similar objects. In choosing among a number of genuine, well-designed, well-made examples, a connoisseur considers objective factors, but often the final choice is based on personal taste of what is beautiful and harmonious. We are often attracted to an object because of its appearance. As we learn more, however, our opinions about the object may change.

Does the aesthetic difference between "city" and "country" interest you? The answer likely will be based on personal opinion. In the marketplace, folk art is highly valued. A painting by an untutored artist may bring as much today as the work of the most refined and sophisticated artists.

Both of the paintings shown here are well known and respected works, but they reflect very different training and talents *(figs. 46, 47)*. Which is more important? The answer is neither; they are different expressions of their time, and both are important.

Appreciation of folk art is growing. The popularity of the work of untrained artisans is evident in the evaluation of two lions *(figs. 48, 49)*. One is a factory product from Vermont and is based on imported English models made in Staffordshire, while the other was hand made by a Pennsylvania craftsman who may never have seen an African lion and who also did not have a factory-made lion figure to copy.

Which is more important? Does the Pennsylvania lion fall short because it is more like a caricature and less lifelike? There are many more examples known of the Vermont lion, and they are available in pairs—one facing the other, for display on a table or mantel. The Vermont lion was probably more costly when it was new, and it would have been used in a stylish city dwelling. The other would have been more at home in a rural setting; it was probably made as a gift by the potter, and it may even have served as a doorstop. Today, the Pennsylvania lion would bring a significantly higher price at auction, but that is not necessarily an objective rating. It is a matter of rarity and the current appreciation of nineteenth-century handmade pottery and folk art.

The Point in Practice

Both of these paintings portray America's first president and hero, George Washington *(figs. 46, 47)*. The one shown in figure 46 was painted in 1790 by John Trumbull (1756–1843). It depicts the arrival of French troops at Verplanck's Point, New York, after the defeat of Lord Cornwallis at Yorktown in 1782.

The portrait in figure 47, from about 1800, is by Frederick Kemmelmeyer. Washington is again depicted in a military scene: the review of militia at Fort Cumberland, Maryland, during the 1794 Whiskey Rebellion—an uprising of western Pennsylvania farmers who were opposed to a federal tax on distilled spirits.

FIG. 46. *WASHINGTON AT VERPLANCK'S POINT*

FIG. 47.
GENERAL GEORGE WASHINGTON REVIEWING THE WESTERN ARMY AT FORT CUMBERLAND

The style of the two paintings and the artistic training of the artists are quite different. Trumbull, who served as an aide to Washington in the Continental Army, resigned his commission to devote his life to painting. In 1780 he studied under Benjamin West in London and was well known for his small-scale paintings. He also produced landscapes and portraits.

Kemmelmeyer, born in Germany, emigrated to the United States in 1788 and became a naturalized citizen in Annapolis the same year. He established a drawing school in Baltimore, which he operated until 1802. He advertised in 1788 that he "paints Miniatures and other sizes, in oil and water colors, and Sign Painting upon moderate terms."

Nothing is known about Kemmelmeyer's training, but judging by the quality of his portraits, it is likely to have been in sign painting rather than portraiture. There is a flat, naive quality to his compositions and brushwork. This depiction of Washington, who died one year before the painting was finished, is a charming painting of the most famous man in America.

Two ceramic lions demonstrate how very different urban and rural crafts can be *(figs. 48, 49)*. The lion in figure 48 was made by John Bell (1800–1880), a potter of Waynesboro, Pennsylvania, between about 1840 and 1880. It is solid (not hollow) and was created by freehand modeling. Bell produced mainly utilitarian objects such as washbowls and pitchers, plates, bowls, cups, and baking dishes. They were made of local cream- or red-colored clay and were decorated with colored slips and lead glazes. The lion was not a piece that was regularly produced but was probably made for a special occasion. A similar lion is said to have been

Fig. 48.
Lion figurine

FIG. 49.
LION FIGURINE

made as a wedding-day gift for Bell's niece. Unfortunately, we do not know anything about this particular lion's history.

The ceramic lion shown in figure 49 was produced in a factory in Bennington, Vermont, between 1849 and 1858. It is made of a more refined earthenware clay that was cast in a full-size mold to form the hollow lion's body, which was applied to a separately molded base. It also has an elegant patented "flint enamel" glaze. The tail and the mane were added by hand.

The lion made by Bell is rare—only four are known—and it has a good-natured, toothy grin. The Vermont lion is more lifelike and businesslike. Given the current favor for folk art in today's market, the Bell lion would probably bring more than ten times as much as the Vermont lion if they were sold. The choice of which to buy, however, is a matter of personal preference.

Final Examination

In terms of craftsmanship and flamboyance, this piece of furniture matches the legendary exploits of a man with the means and will to command the best.

CHARLES F. MONTGOMERY
in *American Furniture: The Federal Period, 1788–1825*

Joseph Barrell built an elegant house, "Pleasant Hill," in Charlestown, near Boston, in 1793. He furnished it with the most fashionable objects available. The house was designed by Charles Bulfinch in the newly popular neoclassical style. Barrell imported many objects from Europe, and he had a greenhouse that was reputed to be two hundred feet long, tended by gardeners from Holland and England.

The desk-and-bookcase shown in figure 50, which displays two different styles, belonged to Barrell. The desk section is rococo; it has swelling, bombé sides, ball-and-claw feet, and chinoiserie brasses. The bookcase is neoclassical and is covered with neoclassical ornaments: an animal head and skulls, ovals, wreaths, and ribbons. It is topped with three carved figures of women, probably representing Justice, Hope, and Commerce *(left to right)*.

The piece has elicited both admiration and suspicion. Does the top really belong to the base? There is no other desk-and-bookcase quite like it. How can it be explained? Could it be that Barrell bought a desk and added a neoclassical bookcase later? Was the original bookcase on Barrell's desk damaged and another made to replace it?

By organizing detailed observations according to Montgomery's fourteen points of connoisseurship, a picture of what may have happened emerges.

Applying the 14 Points of Connoisseurship

1. **OVERALL APPEARANCE:** The Barrell desk-and-bookcase has a bold appearance *(fig. 50)*. The desk section has strong, curved lines. The bookcase has abundant, detailed ornament. There is a noticeable difference in the styles of the top and bottom.

2. **FORM:** Look at the curved line of the pediment. The exaggerated curve is unusual for a bookcase made in Boston in the late eighteenth century. This should lead you to consider that the pediment may not have been designed and constructed when the neoclassical style was first popular in the eighteenth century. Compare it to the pediment on figure 51, another desk-and-bookcase that was made in Boston about the same time.

   The style of the desk section in figures 50a and 50b creates less suspicion. It is a form associated with Boston cabinetmakers working from the 1760s through the 1780s. The similarity of form, proportions, and measurements to those on the desk illustrated in figure 51 suggests that both may have been made in the same shop.

3. **ORNAMENT:** The ornament is skillfully carved, but its arrangement on the bookcase is not well designed; it looks pasted on. The cornice does not continue in a line with the curved pediment (which is expected); the elaborate ram's head is surrounded by plain molding and appears to be added on; the wreaths topping the columns are unusually shaped and

Above left and right:

Fig. 50a. Desk-and-bookcase

Fig. 50b. Open view of desk-and-bookcase

are not integrated with the corners of the mirror frame. These features suggest that the designer or maker was not familiar with the neoclassical style.

4. **MATERIALS:** The lower set of drawer fronts show similar color and wood grain, so they were probably cut from a single lot of mahogany. This practice was typical in the eighteenth century on high-quality furniture and gave the surface a unified appearance. The fact that the wood on the drawer

Above left and right:

FIG. 51a.
DESK-AND-BOOKCASE

FIG. 51b.
DETAIL OF
DESK-AND-BOOKCASE

fronts matches on this desk is not remarkable in itself, however, since the drawers may have been replaced.

5. **FINISH:** No evidence about the early history of the desk-and-bookcase is available from the finish. A cross section of the finish, viewed through a microscope, shows the remains of only two finish layers. That neither one is degraded enough to date from the late 1700s tells us that they are not original. There are many reasons to refinish furniture, but the fact that someone chose to change the object in any way suggests that other changes may have been made as well.

6. **COLOR:** The two sections, desk and bookcase, match each other in color. However, we know that prior to Winterthur's

acquisition of the piece, the desk was stained a darker color to make it match the bookcase. If the two sections had been made at the same time and had always stayed together, they would have undergone the same color changes from exposure to air, accumulation of dirt and polish, and fading in the sunlight. It is suspicious that the desk was lighter than the bookcase.

7. **CRAFT TECHNIQUES:** The construction of the bookcase is unusual, and it suggests that there has been considerable reworking. It seems narrow for the desk and appears to have been cut down from a deeper cabinet. Typically, if the bookcase were original to the desk, it would have been constructed to the full width and depth of the lower case. Also, there is no molding to position the bookcase on top of the desk in figure 50, while there is on the desk in figure 51; in the eighteenth century, bookcases were usually located on the desks with applied moldings.

   Was this bookcase pieced together from another one? The construction details seem to support the thesis that an existing bookcase was altered to produce the one we see now.

8. **TRADE PRACTICES:** The sculpted finials were very finely crafted—by a carver who did not produce any other work on the desk-and-bookcase. Is this suspicious?

   We know that it was common for cabinetmakers to hire specialists for some tasks, particularly for making ornament. Therefore, the unusually high quality of the finials is no proof that they were not originally part of the object—especially in light of the history of ownership of the piece.

9. **FUNCTION:** In order to function as a writing surface, the lid must be supported when it is opened *(fig. 50b)*. This desk has brass hangers that perform that function. However, eighteenth-century desks did not have hangers. Instead, they were built with extendable wood bars, called lopers, that held up the flat writing surfaces.

Evidence on this desk shows that it probably once had lopers. Two filled notches appear inside the top drawer opening. These fills appear to be the remains of dividers that separated the lopers from the top drawer. If lopers were originally present, the front of the top drawer had to be replaced when the lopers were removed since the front had to span the entire width of the opening. Because the wood on all the drawer fronts match, it is probable that all of them were replaced.

10. **STYLE:** The two sections are in different styles. The desk is rococo, or Chippendale, which was fashionable from about 1750 to 1790. The bookcase is neoclassical, or federal, fashionable from about 1785 to 1820.

 Eighteenth-century desk-and-bookcases generally conform to just one style.

11. **ATTRIBUTION:** The desk-and-bookcase shown in figure 51 is so similar in measurement to that in figure 50 that both were probably made using the same templates. (The difference in overall heights is due to the finials; the bombé sections, themselves, are very close in size to each other.) The similarities in profile and construction are close enough to suggest the attribution of the desks to the same maker. Neither desk is signed, but it has been argued that John Cogswell made the desk-and-bookcase illustrated in figure 51 and possibly also the Barrell desk *(fig. 50)*.

12. **HISTORY OF OWNERSHIP:** An engraved brass plaque, probably dating from the late nineteenth century, is mounted inside the bookcase. It is inscribed: "Joseph Barrell / Hannah Barrell Joy (wife of Benjamin Joy) / John Benjamin Joy / Charles Henry Joy / Benjamin Joy," tracing its history through Barrell's daughter and her descendants.

13. **CONDITION:** The desk shows evidence of considerable change. In addition to the drawer fronts on the desk, extra pieces of wood have been spliced onto the sides of the case, and the outside has been planed down and then reinforced from the inside. It may be that the desk sides became warped and the drawer supports came loose and collapsed. Adding wood on the interior to compensate for the warp would facilitate the reconstruction of the case, and extra planing would be required to restore symmetry.

In addition, the interior drawers were probably replaced. The blades separating the drawers have been shortened to accommodate shallower drawers. This change resulted in notches on the inner surfaces of the desk sides. Faint scribe lines also indicate that the fronts of the original drawers were at a very different slope.

14. **EVALUATION:** This object has typical characteristics of the desk-and-bookcase form at the end of the eighteenth century. The bookcase has a pediment, interior shelves, and flanking pilasters. The desk has a slant front, small drawers flanking a central door, and graduated exterior drawers.

It also has distinctive qualities. These include an unusual combination of styles: a neoclassical bookcase, a rococo desk; bombé sides combined with a serpentine front; exuberant ornament on the bookcase; and finely carved finials.

This desk-and-bookcase might have appeal as a sophisticated eighteenth-century furniture form with some unusual features. Some connoisseurs might find the difference in style between top and bottom appealing; others might find it jarring and suspicious.

CONCLUSION: When experts judge a piece of furniture, or any other object, they examine all the available evidence and consider many possible explanations for it. Often, as with this desk-and-bookcase, there is no single explanation that accounts for all the evidence. Which explanation do you choose?

1. Joseph Barrell ordered a desk-and-bookcase about the time he built his dramatic new home near Boston. The original bookcase was later damaged, and another was made. Its design was different from the original, but the finials were saved and reused. This explanation is supported by: color, trade practices, attribution, and history of ownership.

2. After many years, Barrell's desk-and-bookcase became old-fashioned, and its condition deteriorated. In the late nineteenth century, when earlier "colonial" furniture styles became popular again, the desk was repaired. Someone created a colonial revival bookcase, perhaps using remnants of the original, removed the lopers, added the brass hangers, and replaced all the drawer fronts on the desk. This explanation is supported by: form, ornament, materials, craft techniques, and function.

3. Barrell ordered the desk in the late 1700s. He later decided to add a bookcase to it, which was converted from another. The styles of the sections differ because fashion had changed by the time he ordered the new bookcase. This explanation is supported by: style and history of ownership.

So far, there is no single explanation that satisfies all of the observations. The Barrell desk-and-bookcase remains an enigma, but the connoisseurship principles enunciated by Charles Montgomery in 1961 do help us to come closer to the truth.

GLOSSARY

CHAIR

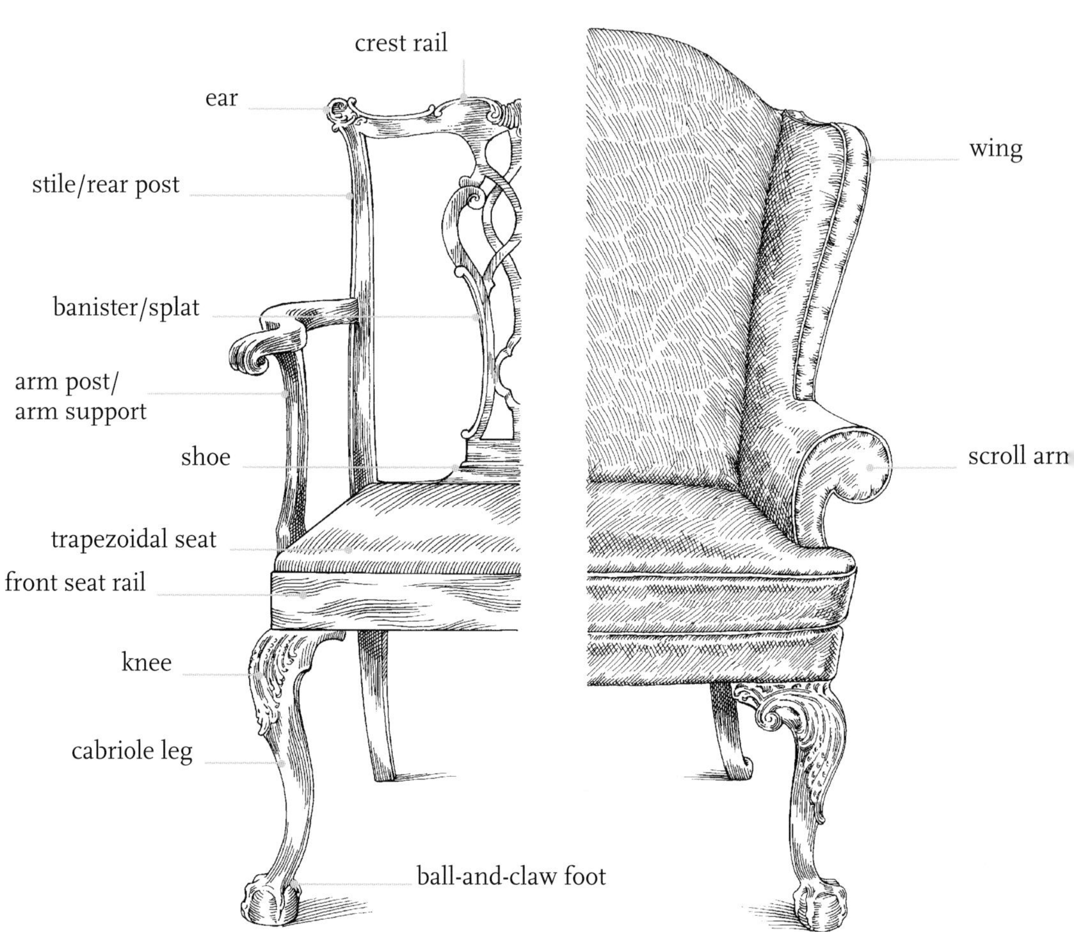
Armchair
Easy chair
crest rail
ear
stile/rear post
banister/splat
arm post/
arm support
shoe
trapezoidal seat
front seat rail
knee
cabriole leg
ball-and-claw foot
wing
scroll arm

CASE PIECE

DESK-AND-BOOKCASE

CHEST-ON-CHEST

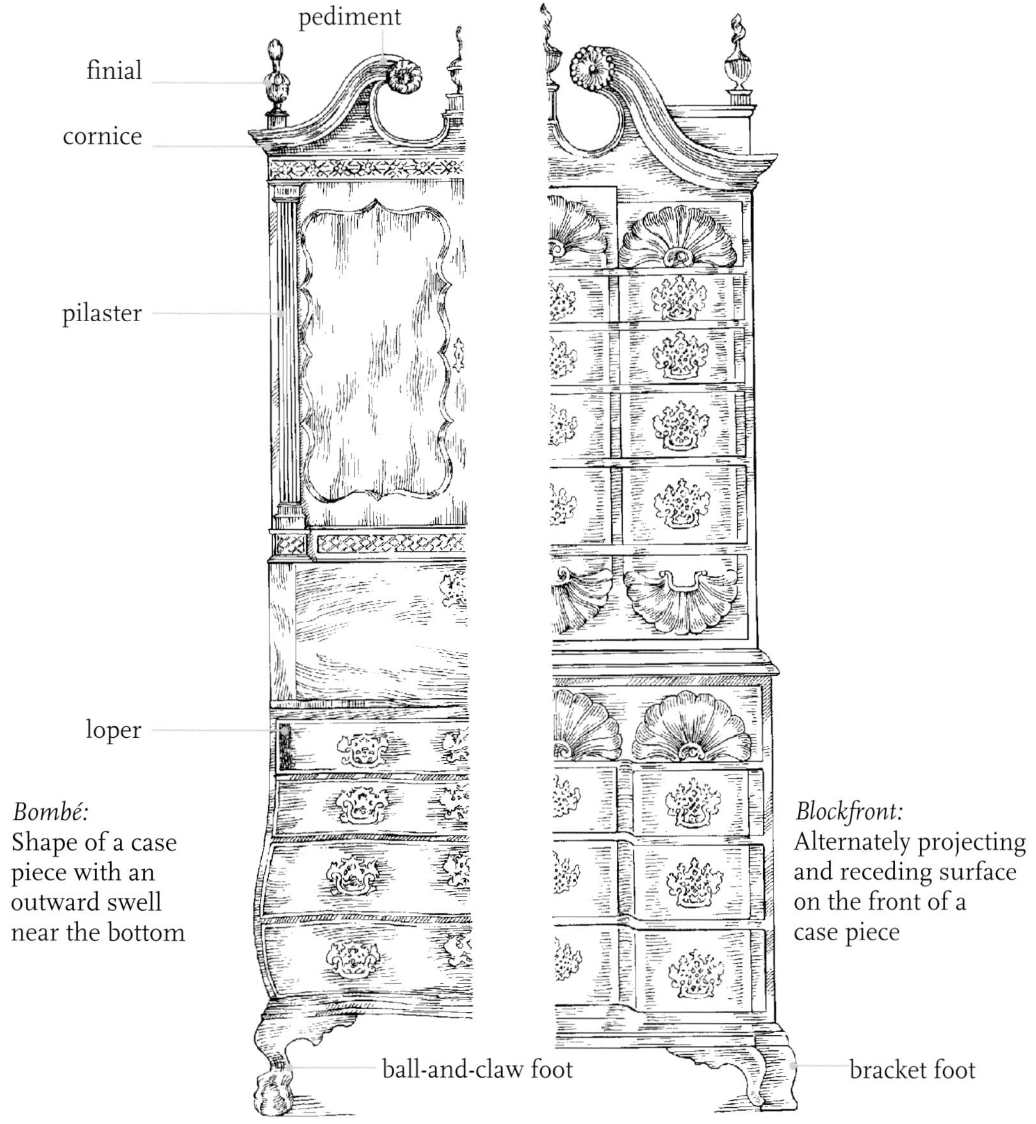

Bombé:
Shape of a case piece with an outward swell near the bottom

Blockfront:
Alternately projecting and receding surface on the front of a case piece

SUGGESTED READINGS

GENERAL REFERENCE

Fleming, John, and Hugh Honour. *The Penguin Dictionary of Decorative Arts.* New York: Viking Penguin, 1989.

AMERICANA

Cantor, Jay E. *Winterthur. The Foremost Museum of American Furniture and Decorative Arts.* Expanded and updated. New York: Harry N. Abrams, 1997.

Hummel, Charles F., and Beatrice B. Garvan. *The Pennsylvania Germans: A Celebration of Their Arts, 1683–1850.* Philadelphia: Philadelphia Museum of Art, 1982.

Kirk, John T. *The Shaker World: Art, Life, Belief.* New York: Harry N. Abrams, 1997.

Mayhew, Edgar de Noailles, and Minor Myers, Jr. *A Documentary History of American Interiors from the Colonial Era to 1915.* New York: Charles Scribner's Sons, 1980.

Nineteenth-Century America: Furniture and Other Decorative Arts. New York: Metropolitan Museum of Art, 1970.

CERAMICS

Denker, Bert, and Ellen Denker. *The Main Street Pocket Guide to North American Pottery and Porcelain.* Pittstown, N.J.: Main Street Press, 1985.

Frelinghuysen, Alice Cooney. *American Porcelain, 1770–1920.* New York: Metropolitan Museum of Art, 1989.

Levin, Elaine. *The History of American Ceramics, 1607 to the Present: From Pipkins and Beanpots to Contemporary Forms.* New York: Harry N. Abrams, 1988.

Lewis, Griselda. *A Collector's History of English Pottery.* 4th ed. Woodbridge, Suffolk, Eng.: Antique Collectors' Club, 1987.

Savage, George, and Harold Newman. *An Illustrated Dictionary of Ceramics.* Rev. ed. London: Thames and Hudson, 1989.

FURNITURE

Bates, Elizabeth Bidwell, and Jonathan Fairbanks. *American Furniture, 1620 to the Present.* New York: Richard Marek, 1981.

Fitzgerald, Oscar P. *Four Centuries of American Furniture.* Radnor, Pa.: Wallace-Homestead Book Co., 1995.

Gloag, John. *A Complete Dictionary of Furniture.* Rev. and exp. by Clive Edwards. Woodstock, N.Y.: Overlook Press, 1991.

Kaye, Myrna. *Fake, Fraud, or Genuine? Identifying Authentic American Antique Furniture.* Boston: Little, Brown, 1987.

Sack, Albert. *The New Fine Points of Furniture: Early American, Good, Better, Best, Superior, Masterpiece.* New York: Crown Publishing, 1993.

GLASS

Charleston, Robert J. *Masterpieces of Glass: A World History from the Corning Museum of Glass.* New York: Harry N. Abrams, 1980.

Newman, Harold. *An Illustrated Dictionary of Glass.* London: Thames and Hudson, 1977.

Palmer, Arlene. *Glass in Early America: Selections from the Henry Francis du Pont Winterthur Museum.* Winterthur, Del.: Henry Francis du Pont Winterthur Museum, 1993.

Wilson, Kenneth M., and Helen McKearin. *American Bottles and Flasks and Their Ancestry.* New York: Crown Publishing, 1978.

Zerwick, Chloe. *A Short History of Glass.* Corning, N.Y.: Corning Museum of Glass, 1990.

METALWORK

Coffin, Margaret. *The History and Folklore of American Country Tinware, 1700–1900.* Camden, N.J.: Thomas Nelson and Sons, 1968.

Fennimore, Donald L. *Metalwork in Early America: Copper and Its Alloys from the Winterthur Collection.* Winterthur, Del.: Henry Francis du Pont Winterthur Museum, 1996.

Montgomery, Charles F. *A History of American Pewter*. Rev. and enl. New York: E. P. Dutton, 1978.

Schiffer, Herbert, Peter Schiffer, and Nancy Schiffer. *Antique Iron: Survey of American and English Forms, Fifteenth through Nineteenth Centuries*. Exton, Pa.: Schiffer Publishing, 1979.

Gentle, Rupert, and Rachael Feild. *Domestic Metalwork, 1640–1820*. Rev. and enl. by Belinda Gentle. Woodbridge, Suffolk, Eng.: Antique Collectors' Club, 1994.

PAINTINGS AND PRINTS

Fowble, E. McSherry. *Two Centuries of Prints in America, 1680–1880: A Selective Catalogue of the Winterthur Museum Collection*. Winterthur, Del.: Henry Francis du Pont Winterthur Museum, 1987.

Griffiths, Antony. *Prints and Printmaking: An Introduction to the History and Techniques*. Berkeley and Los Angeles: University of California Press, 1996.

Groce, George Cuthbert, and David H. Wallace. *New-York Historical Society's Dictionary of Artists in America, 1564–1860*. New Haven: Yale University Press, 1957.

Lipman, Jean, and Tom Armstrong, eds. *American Folk Painters of Three Centuries*. New York: Whitney Museum of American Art, 1980.

Prown, Jules David, and Barbara Rose. *American Painting: From the Colonial Period to the Present*. Rev. ed. Introduction by John Walker. New York: Rizzoli, 1977.

SILVER

Ensko, Stephen Guernsey Cook. *American Silversmiths and Their Marks IV*. Rev. and enl. ed. compiled by Dorothea Ensko Wyle. Boston: David R. Godine, 1988.

Newman, Harold. *An Illustrated Dictionary of Silverware*. London: Thames and Hudson, 1987.

Quimby, Ian M. G., with Dianne Johnson. *American Silver at Winterthur*. Winterthur, Del.: Henry Francis du Pont Winterthur Museum, 1995.

Venable, Charles L. *Silver in America, 1840–1940: A Century of Splendor*. Dallas: Dallas Museum of Art, 1994.

Wees, Beth Carver. *English, Irish, and Scottish Silver at the Sterling and Francine Clark Art Institute*. New York: Hudson Hills Press, 1997.

TEXTILES AND FABRICS

Brackman, Barbara. *Clues in the Calico: A Guide to Identifying and Dating Antique Quilts.* McLean, Va.: EPM Publications, 1989.

Burnham, Dorothy K. *Warp and Weft: A Textile Terminology.* Toronto: Royal Ontario Museum, 1980.

Cooke, Edward S., Jr., et al. *Upholstery in America and England: From the Seventeenth Century to World War I.* New York: W. W. Norton, 1987.

Schoeser, Mary, and Celia Rufey. *English and American Textiles: From 1790 to the Present.* New York: Thames and Hudson, 1989.

Swan, Susan Burrows. *Plain and Fancy: American Women and Their Needlework, 1650–1850.* Rev. ed. Austin, Tex.: Curious Works Press, 1995.

LIST OF ILLUSTRATIONS

FIG. 9.
PITCHER
Possibly Boston and Sandwich Glass Company, England, 1820–40
Lead glass
H. 6 1/2", Diam. (base) 3 1/2"
59.3221 Gift of Henry Francis du Pont

FIG. 10.
TANKARD/PITCHER
Philadelphia, Joseph and Nathaniel Richardson, 1787 and twentieth century
Silver
H. 8 1/16", W. 7 3/4"
76.71 Gift of Richard Wistar

CHAPTER 3

FIG. 11.
CHEST OF DRAWERS WITH THREE SHELLS
Probably Colchester, Connecticut, 1770–90
Cherry, white pine, tulip-poplar
H. 37", W. 40", D. 19"
64.664 Gift of Henry Francis du Pont

FIG. 12.
CHEST OF DRAWERS WITH NINE SHELLS
New England, in the style of Connecticut, probably late nineteenth century
Cherry, white pine
H. 33", W. 36", D. 19"
57.507 Bequest of Henry Francis du Pont

FIG. 13. *Left to right:*
POCKET BOTTLE
Attributed to the glassworks of Henry William Stiegel, Manheim, Pennsylvania, 1769–74
Colorless nonlead glass
H. 4 3/16", W. 3 1/8"
59.3088 Gift of Henry Francis du Pont

POCKET BOTTLE
Attributed to the glassworks of Henry William Stiegel, Manheim, Pennsylvania, 1769–74
Light blue nonlead glass
H. 5 1/4", W. 3 3/4"
59.3131 Gift of Henry Francis du Pont

POCKET BOTTLE
Attributed to the glassworks of Henry William Stiegel, Manheim, Pennsylvania, 1769–74
Amethyst nonlead glass
H. 4 3/4", W. 3 1/2"
59.3144 Gift of Henry Francis du Pont

POCKET BOTTLE
Probably Czechoslovakia, 1915–30
Amethyst nonlead glass
H. 6", W. 4"
59.3113 Gift of Henry Francis du Pont

CHAPTER 4

FIG. 14a.
SIDE CHAIR
Philadelphia, ca. 1875
Red oak, maple, ash, white oak, mahogany
H. 39 5/8", W. 22 1/2", D. 17 3/4"
63.34 Gift of James Biddle

FIG. 14b.
DETAIL OF OAK SIDE CHAIR

FIG. 15.
SIDE CHAIR
Thomas Tufft (labeled), Philadelphia, 1760–80
Mahogany, white cedar
H. 38 7/8", W. 23 3/4", D. 21 3/8"
57.514 Gift of Henry Francis du Pont

Fig. 16.
Caster
Peter Van Dyck, New York City, 1729–50 and twentieth century
Silver
H. 3 1/4", W. 2 5/16"
58.2104 Gift of Henry Francis du Pont

CHAPTER 5

Fig. 17.
Bureau table
Attributed to Edmund Townsend, Newport, Rhode Island, ca. 1780
Mahogany, chestnut, hard pine[?]
H. 33", W. 36 1/4", D. 20 1/2"
Sotheby's, New York

Fig. 18.
Bureau table
Attributed to Newport, Rhode Island, 1750–70
Mahogany, chestnut, hard pine[?]
H. 34 1/2", W. 39", D. 20 1/4"
Christie's Images

Fig. 19.
Teakettle, stand, and burner
England, probably London, 1730–60
Copper, tin, rattan
H. 14", W. 9 13/16"
59.4.4 Museum purchase, funds given by Henry Francis du Pont

CHAPTER 6

Fig. 20a.
Needlework picture
Priscilla Allen, Boston, 1746
Linen, wool, silk
H. 21", W. 15 3/8"
62.588 Bequest of Henry Francis du Pont

Fig. 20b.
Reverse of needlework picture

Fig. 21.
Drawer from a chamber table
Boston, 1800–1810
Mahogany, birch, rosewood, white pine
57.1007 Bequest of Henry Francis du Pont

Fig. 22.
Drawer from a washstand
Philadelphia, 1900–1950 (bearing an eighteenth-century label of John Elliott)
Mahogany, maple, hard pine
69.1677 Bequest of Henry Francis du Pont

CHAPTER 7

Fig. 23.
Left: Flagon
Attributed to William Will, Philadelphia, 1785–98
Pewter
H. 13 15/16", W. 7 1/2"
58.649 Gift of Henry Francis du Pont

Center: Coffeepot
William Will, Philadelphia, 1785–98
Pewter, wood
H. 15 9/16", W. 13 1/4"
55.624 Gift of Henry Francis du Pont

Right: Coffeepot
William Will, Philadelphia, 1785–98
Pewter, wood
H. 15 7/8", W. 11 3/8"
54.33 Gift of Henry Francis du Pont

FIG. 24.
PLATES
Bearing the marks of Thomas Danforth III, ca. 1969
Pewter
H. 5/8", Diam. 7 3/4"
69.203 Gift of Dr. Donald M. Herr *(left)*; collection of Dr. Donald M. Herr *(right)*

CHAPTER 8

FIG. 25.
COUCH
Bearing the label of Thomas Needham, Jr., of Salem, Massachusetts
China, ca. 1820
Mahogany and aspen
H. 30 3/4", W. 71 1/2", D. 25 3/4"
57.575 Gift of Henry Francis du Pont

FIG. 26.
TULIPS
Engraved by Richard Earlom
From Robert John Thornton, *Temple of Flora* (London, 1807)
Page: H. 22 1/8", W. 17 1/8"
RBR QK92 T51 PFF Winterthur Library, gift of the Friends of Winterthur

CHAPTER 9

FIG. 27.
TEAPOT
England, 1730–45
Lead glass
H. 6 3/16", W. 8 1/16", D. 4 1/2"
81.0067 Museum purchase

FIG. 28.
"SPICE" CHEST
Philadelphia, 1695–1725
Walnut, cedar, oak, yellow pine
H. 32 15/16", W. 21", D. 9 1/2"
88.132 Gift of Mrs. Winifred C. Beer; Dr. Jane D. Cadbury; John W. Cadbury III; Elizabeth C. Musgrave; Catherine C. Lambe; Christopher J. Cadbury; B. Bartram Cadbury; Joel B. Cadbury; Lloyd Cadbury; Emma Cadbury; Warder H. Cadbury; and David F. Cadbury, all the cousins of Mary Hoxie Jones.

CHAPTER 10

FIG. 29.
PILGRIM CENTURY GREAT CHAIR
Boston, 1650–75
Soft maple, poplar, ash (replacement)
H. 44 1/2", W. 24 1/2", D. 21 3/4"
58.681 Gift of Henry Francis du Pont

FIG. 30.
WILLIAM AND MARY ARMCHAIR
Boston, 1720–30
American maple
H. 49 7/8", W. 24 1/4", D. 21"
54.528b Gift of Henry Francis du Pont

FIG. 31.
QUEEN ANNE ARMCHAIR
Boston, 1735–45
Soft maple, American black walnut
H. 43 5/8", W. 24", D. 23 1/4"
59.69a Gift of Henry Francis du Pont

FIG. 32.
CHIPPENDALE ARMCHAIR
Boston, 1765–80
Mahogany, hard maple
H. 38 1/2", W. 29", D. 24 1/2"
52.234a Gift of Henry Francis du Pont

Fig. 33.
Neoclassical armchair
Salem, Massachusetts, carving attributed to Samuel McIntire, 1796–1800
H. 38", W. 22", D. 18 3/8"
57.691 Gift of Henry Francis du Pont

Fig. 34. *Left to right:*
Drinking glass
Probably Venice (Murano), 1660–80
Nonlead glass
H. 6 1/4", Diam. (bowl) 3 9/16"
75.205 Museum purchase, funds gift of the Claneil Foundation

Drinking glass
England, 1690–1710
Lead glass
H. 14 1/2", Diam. (bowl) 8 7/8"
63.685 Museum purchase

Drinking glass
England, 1725–40
Lead glass
H. 6 3/8", Diam. (bowl) 2 13/16"
68.116 Museum purchase

Drinking glass
England, enameled decoration attributed to the shop of William Beilby, Newcastle upon Tyne, ca. 1765
Lead glass
H. 6 3/8", Diam. (bowl) 2 11/16"
75.44.1 Museum purchase through trade

Drinking glass
England, 1770–90
Lead glass
H. 6 3/4", Diam. (bowl) 2 1/8"
68.167 Gift of Mrs. Hugh W. Kelly

CHAPTER II

Fig. 35.
Side chair
Probably New York City, ca. 1850; bearing a fake label of J. H. Belter and Company
Mahogany
H. 36 5/8", W. 18 3/4", D. 24 3/4"
90.81 Gift of Richard and Eileen Dubrow

Fig. 36.
Label on side chair

Fig. 37.
Sgraffito plate
George Hübener (signed), Upper Hanover Township, Montgomery County, Pennsylvania, dated 1786
Earthenware, lead glaze
H. 2 1/8", Diam. 12 1/2"
Philadelphia Museum of Art, gift of John T. Morris

Fig. 38.
Sgraffito plate
Attributed to George Hübener, Upper Hanover Township, Montgomery County, Pennsylvania, dated 1789
Earthenware, lead glaze
H. 2 1/4", Diam. 13"
65.2301 Bequest of Henry Francis du Pont

Fig. 39.
Sgraffito plate
Attributed to George Hübener, Upper Hanover Township, Montgomery County, Pennsylvania, dated 1787
Earthenware, lead glaze
H. 2", Diam. 13 11/16"
65.2300 Bequest of Henry Francis du Pont

CHAPTER 12

Fig. 40.
Armchair
New York, Long Island, probably Huntington, 1720–40
White oak, soft maple, red cedar, hickory
H. 54 13/16", W. 30 9/16", D. 17 13/16"
88.3 Museum purchase, Collectors Circle funds

Fig. 41.
Tankard (one of a set of six)
Paul Revere, Jr., Boston, 1772
Silver
H. 8 1/4", W. 6 11/16", Diam. (base) 4 7/8"
57.859.1 Gift of Henry Francis du Pont

Fig. 42.
Set of six tankards
Paul Revere, Jr., Boston, 1772
Silver
57.859.1–6 Gift of Henry Francis du Pont

CHAPTER 13

Fig. 43.
Windsor high chair
Pennsylvania, 1765–1810
Tulip-poplar, maple, ash, oak
H. 40 1/4", W. 18 1/4"
64.924 Gift of Henry Francis du Pont

Fig. 44.
Windsor high chair
Wallace Nutting, Framingham, Massachusetts, 1920–35
White pine, birch, oak
H. 37", W. 15 1/8"
58.635a Gift of Henry Francis du Pont

Fig. 45.
Left: Coffeepot
Probably Pennsylvania, 1830–60 or later
Tin-plated iron, paint
H. 10 1/2"
59.2027 Gift of Henry Francis du Pont

Right: Coffeepot
Pennsylvania, possibly Philadelphia, ca. 1875
Tin-plated iron, asphaltum, paint
H. 10 3/4"
65.1599 Gift of Henry Francis du Pont

CHAPTER 14

Fig. 46.
Washington at Verplanck's Point
John Trumbull (signed), New York, 1790
Oil on canvas
H. 30", W. 20 1/8"
64.2201 Gift of Henry Francis du Pont

Fig. 47.
General George Washington Reviewing the Western Army at Fort Cumberland
Frederick Kemmelmeyer, Baltimore, ca. 1800
Oil on paper
H. 18 1/8", W. 23 1/8"
58.2780 Bequest of Henry Francis du Pont

Fig. 48.
Lion figurine
John Bell, Waynesboro, Pennsylvania, 1840–80
Earthenware, lead glaze
H. 7 3/8", W. 8 1/2"
67.1630 Gift of Henry Francis du Pont

Fig. 49.
Lion figurine
Lyman, Fenton and Company, Bennington, Vermont, 1849–58
Earthenware, lead glaze
H. 9 1/4", W. 10 13/16", D. 5 3/4"
67.1874 Gift of Henry Francis du Pont

CHAPTER 15

Fig. 50a.
Desk-and-bookcase
Boston-Salem area, 1785–1800, with late nineteenth-century alterations
Mahogany, white pine group
H. 95 1/2", W. (upper case) 31 7/16", W. (bombé) 36 15/16", D. (bombé) 19 3/8"
56.23 Gift of Henry Francis du Pont

Fig. 50b.
Open view of desk-and-bookcase

Fig. 51a.
Desk-and-bookcase
Boston, 1780–95
Mahogany, white pine group, yellow pine group
H. 82 1/16", W. (upper case) 33 1/2", W. (bombé) 36 5/8", D. (bombé) 19 13/16"
57.1396 Gift of Henry Francis du Pont

Fig. 51b.
Detail of desk-and-bookcase